KEARNEY

How to hack your supply chain

Breaking today, building tomorrow

Dr. Elouise Epstein

Foreword by Rachel Kutz

KEARNEY

This book is dedicated to my wife Denise, our hounds, my Kearney colleagues, and the supply chain profession—thank you for putting up with me.

Table of contents

Table of contents (continued)

Figures

Figures (continued)

Foreword

Like Dr. Epstein, I think about supply chains all the time. They are increasingly complex and scary, whether you're managing supply chains, working alongside them, or relying on one as a customer.

In fact, I rely on experiences as the latter—a customer—to inform how I approach supply chain in my work. I try to think like the customer, whether that's internal clients or external buyers of our products. Questions such as "How do customers use our products and services?" and "How are they most likely to shop?" fill my head. In many cases, I'm a customer too. So, what are my pain points? What makes me happy? How do I get my stuff?

I didn't start my career in supply chain, but my desire to get even closer to customers led me there from previous roles in technical operations. In 2009, I joined supply chain at a Fortune 50 company, leading teams responsible for product sourcing, planning, and quality. I also helmed teams responsible for product logistics, distribution, fulfillment, and reverse. And finally, after working in nearly every part of the supply chain (minus "make"), I moved into a role heading up supply chain strategy initiatives, which included digital procurement transformation, risk management enhancement, and ESG implementation.

Of course, COVID upended everything. Like every other supply chain leader, I went foraging for personal protective equipment, and fought daily to keep sellable products on the shelves as the global market constricted. These days, I'm implementing omnichannel transformation and—ironically—cleaning out inventory levels that are too high due to all the great work we did to keep products in stock.

While reading Dr. Epstein's first book, *Trade Wars, Pandemics, and Chaos*, I thought to myself: *here's someone who thinks differently*. This is someone who doesn't use the same jargon as all the other consultants who are trying to sell the next best thing (blockchain, anyone?). I was especially intrigued by her thoughts on digital transformation and the spider map. My only disappointment was that she published her book after I implemented my company's digital transformation. Still, her words and ideas gave voice to what I experienced and the challenges I encountered. I was introduced to Dr. Epstein shortly afterward, and I felt like a little kid meeting a celebrity.

In this book, Dr. Epstein examines the supply chain again, digging into the new challenges facing all businesses. We were both struck by the paradox of our supply chain reality during the pandemic, staring down at our vaccination record cards after getting immunized and thinking, "Is this tiny bit of paper the thing I now must protect most dearly? Is this really the best process we can develop in the digital age?"

The ideas presented in this book are thoughtful, intriguing, and frightening— Dr. Epstein touches on the things that keep us, as supply chain leaders, up at night. Her book, however, thrusts these issues into the light and explains why they should command our attention. We must face supply chain challenges head-on, even if they seem too complex or overwhelming to address. Supplier management and the risks suppliers pose to our businesses are real. ESG, even in the current political climate, creates the need for businesses to understand exactly how products are sourced, manufactured, and delivered. And as always, good data governance and maintenance remain key.

Dr. Epstein's writing is approachable, and her examples and analogies make for an enjoyable, thought-provoking, and accessible read. Even more importantly, this book brings the current supply chain challenges to the surface and gives foundational understanding so that we can begin to create solutions. For example, I've already shifted my mindset to a "left-of-boom" approach, which will ensure my organization has the capabilities to navigate whatever complexities the future holds. We may not have all the answers, but this book helps us ask the right questions so that we can find them. I found it extremely helpful, and I'm now recommending this book to not just supply chain professionals but to all leaders looking to make their businesses more secure, sustainable, and resilient.

Rachel Kutz

Supply Chain Operations Leader

Acknowledgments

This book is an amalgamation of thousands of conversations, debates, and presentations over the past couple years. It would not have been possible without the generous contributions of many people.

First, I would like to thank Rachel Kutz for contributing such a splendid and thoughtful foreword to this book. Working with someone as esteemed and experienced as Rachel is deeply gratifying and is why I love my job so much. Words can hardly describe how appreciative I am to be able to work with supply chain leaders like her.

I am equally grateful to JD Ambati, Emal Ehsan, Arshita Raju, Guilherme Silberstein, and Lance Younger for graciously contributing materials, feedback, and ideas for this book.

I am indebted to Ninian Wilson, Reinhard Plaza Bartsch, and Sabih Rozales along with Dhriti Adhikary, Sanran Gulsen, and the entire Vodafone Procurement Company team for happily welcoming me into their world and introducing me to the beauty of Luxembourg.

I am especially appreciative to Mike Cadieux, Gillis Jonk, Tom Kiely, Mike Schiappa, Fulden Sener, Conrad Smith, and Jason Tham for kindly reading and commenting on the manuscript. This book is better because of their feedback.

My sincere gratitude to my colleagues John Blascovich, Mark Clouse, Ana Conde, Remko de Bruijn, Suketu Ghandi, Jeff Hewitt, Tiffany Hickerson,

Tom Kline, Shakil Nathoo, Joel Saldana, Balika Sonthalia, Dr. Michael Strohmer, Yves Thill, Jane Wanklyn, and Ana Maria Yamakami.

Once again, Emily Deng deserves a standing ovation for her tireless dedication and work to organize and support the creation of this book.

I want to highlight the yeoman's effort put in by my editor Kelly Kearsley to provide a much-needed semblance of structure and readability to this manuscript.

I would like to recognize the contributions of Haley Dunbrack, Briana Flosi, Kerry MacKenzie, Jack May, and the Kearney production team for producing and bringing this book to life.

I am thankful to Charlie Clark, Steve Comstock, Adam Crawley, Nil Difur, Karoline Dygas, Stephen Easton, Robin Evans, Johan Gott, Edenize Maron Gundim, Donna Hagerman, Pam Heminger, Patrick Magloin, Lynne McDonnell, Christian Schuh, Detlef Schultz, Pallaw Sharma, Brian Smith, Bindiya Vakil, and Peter Weis for countless discussions, answering of questions, and/or moments of inspiration.

A special mention to Sarah Elovich, my public-speaking coach, who has helped me shape and refine this material through my presentations.

A shout-out to Nefesh Mountain, whose melodic bluegrass folk music kept me methodically focused on writing.

I am deeply appreciative to entrepreneur and Digital Procurement World founder Matthias Gutzmann for generously agreeing to launch my book at his event and for serving as a role model for entrepreneurship.

Finally, no list of recognition would be complete without giving significant credit to my lovely and immensely talented wife Dr. Denise Dávila whose immeasurable support is the greatest gift. As a literacy professor her influence and inspiration are reflected throughout Chapter V, *People: preparing practitioners for the digital zeitgeist*. Also, a special mention to our hound brigade who ensure I get out into nature, where many ideas come to light.

Chapter I
The vaccine story

"The past is your lesson. The present is your gift. The future is your motivation."

– Anonymous

Let's go back to March 23, 2021—the day that launched the idea for this book. I'm sitting on an uncomfortable plastic chair in a Walmart superstore in Henderson, NV, waiting the obligatory 15 minutes after my first COVID-19 vaccine shot. I've been staring intently at the small square of paper in my hand—my vaccine record card. I keep reading it over and over, fixated on the sparse bits of information on the page. There's my name, date of birth, the date, store number, and the Moderna batch number. While I didn't experience any side effects from the vaccine during that waiting period, I did have an existential crisis about the future.

My short- and long-term health outlook depended on this small piece of paper, which I would need to hold onto for the next four weeks until I could get my second dose. Where do I store the paper so it's safe and I can also find it? I'm good at hiding important documents to keep them secure. Unfortunately, I'm not as good at retrieving said documents; the locations are so secure that I often forget where I hid them. Now I have to hold onto this paper indefinitely until I get the information to my primary healthcare provider, insurance provider, employer, and potentially various government entities. (See Figure 1: *Vaccine card* on page 2.)

Figure 1
Vaccine card

COVID-19 Vaccination Record Card				
Please keep this record card, which includes medical information about the vaccines you have received.				CDC
Por favor, guarde esta tarjeta de registro, que incluye información médica sobre las vacunas que ha recibido.				

Last Name: *Epstein*	First Name: *Elouise*			MI
Date of birth		Patient number *(medical record or IIS record number)*		

Vaccine	Product Name/Manufacturer Lot Number	Date	Healthcare Professional or Clinic Site
1st Dose COVID-19	Moderno 002B21A	3 /23/21 mm dd yy	LoM # 2050
2nd Dose COVID-19	Moderna 043B21A	4 /21/21 mm dd yy	wm 2050
Other		__/__/__ mm dd yy	
Other		__/__/__ mm dd yy	

Source: Elouise Epstein

My fixation on this small slip of paper led to questions about the provenance of the vaccine now coursing through my veins. I started to wonder, where did Moderna batch #002B21A come from? Was it stored at the proper temperature throughout the chain of custody? Was it handled properly once received? What ingredients went into it, and where did they originate from? I started wondering how many various entities touched this vaccine dose from the time it came off the production line until the time it was injected into my arm. None of these questions could I answer.

That's the moment I had two diametrically opposed thoughts. First, I panicked as I realized the American healthcare infrastructure is an absolute disaster. I can have my contact information, all my transportation tickets, and my banking in a digital wallet on my phone. Yet for my health and livelihood, I must carry my proof of vaccination on a piece of physical paper. I know electronic health records (EHRs) have been around for quite a while, yet the two aren't remotely connected. And supply chain traceability has been around for an equally significant amount of time. Am I supposed to accept that this is how we manage supply chain information? This led to my second realization. At that moment, I realized that the problems plaguing the healthcare system weren't unique to healthcare. I came to appreciate that we need to collectively reimagine how we design, build, and operate supply chains. This book sets out to determine why we're operating in a disconnected and archaic fashion that makes our supply chains decidedly insecure—and, most importantly, how we change.

When I started writing this book in the summer of 2021, we'd just had two ships beached in the Suez Canal, ongoing labor shortages, the threat of dock worker strikes, the semiconductor shortage, ships stuck off the coast of LA, and the start of the Great Resignation. Each month brought another disruption of some sort. By the summer of 2022, supply chains were backlogged due to China's zero COVID policy, a potential American West Coast dock worker strike, inflation, a somewhat debatable recession, continued labor shortages, and logistics capacity constraints. This was on top of Russia's invasion of Ukraine, which though not a supply chain disruption (see Chapter VII sidebar on page 116: *Why wars are not supply chain disruptions*), has put additional pressure on global markets. And this doesn't even account for the global climate crisis. By the time this book has gone to print, there will undoubtedly be more disruptions to add to the list. In fact, I argue that we'll go bouncing along from disruption to disruption for the next 10 years.

Today's supply chain problems were created by decisions made in the late 1990s through the 2010s. During this time, the world was a fairly stable place, at least for conducting trade in a globalized market. As a result, many of the preferred strategies enacted squeezed cost and maximized profit by extending global supply chains. Naturally, this created brittle and fault-intolerant supply chains that are primed for security breaches. The goal of this book is not to critique whether these were good or bad decisions; historians and future scholars can tackle those questions. The issue now is how we fix the problems systematically and for the long term. How do we take the steps today to build a safer, more sustainable 21st century supply chain?

What are we doing?

At the end of 2019, I was approached by a client who wanted to engage Kearney to help them negotiate with their systems integrator (SI). For their "future supply chain," they wanted to consolidate their 10 enterprise resource planning (ERP) systems down to a single big ERP system because they are "a big ERP shop." They had selected big SI as their SI partner because they viewed big SI as their "corporate SI." Unfortunately, the project was already four months behind schedule and $96 million over budget. And the worst part? The implementation hadn't started.

While I am not a negotiation expert, I do know that if you are unwilling to switch technologies or SIs, you won't be able to negotiate $96 million off your price. Of course, once the implementation started, the project was further delayed, and the budget overages piled up. This company has approximately $5 billion in annual revenue and a market cap of $8.5 billion—so not exactly a financial juggernaut. If this is the best that the collective "we" can do to create a digital supply chain, we should just stop what we're doing and walk away. But I don't believe it's the best we can do. I'm pretty certain that there's another, better way to hack our supply chains, escape the oppression of old technology and subpar implementation, and move toward a system that's more secure and better equipped for the future.

Why this book, why now?

I was motivated to write this book for three reasons. First, I wanted to continue the story from my first book, *Trade Wars, Pandemics, and Chaos: How Digital Procurement Enables Business Success in a Disordered World*. Second, I made an error I wanted to correct in that book. Third, while supply chains have become common topics in public discourse, I continually ask myself, "What is a supply chain?"

Reason #1: My moment of clarity

Some readers may be familiar with my previous book. As I was writing the last few pages, I had an epiphany. It occurred to me that supply chains have become increasingly externalized. If you look at the end-to-end supply chain, it is predominantly a series of third-party entities from contract manufacturers, co-packers, and third-party logistics providers (3PLs) to the myriad direct and indirect suppliers who provide the necessary materials and services. Once we look at supply chains as a conglomeration of third-party entities, we can start to see what we didn't see before. For fans of the *Matrix* movie, this is the moment when Neo recognizes the matrix as a simulated reality that he can manipulate.

If supply chains are simply an amalgamation of third-party entities, then they are at significant risk. The number of third parties touching the packages, pallets of packages, and containers of pallets is staggering. Each third party and the corresponding handoff introduces risk. Even non-product supply chains (such as banking or software), while not tracking physical goods from here to there, still have many third parties they are engaging with. More succinctly, the greatest risk to the supply chain comes through third parties. The more third parties, the more difficulty managing them and subsequently greater risk. Conversely, the greatest ESG and innovation opportunities come through third parties.

At the heart of these third-party risks and opportunities is the need for sophisticated data exchange and digital competency.

This represents a fundamental recalibration of the supply chain management profession. To run a modern supply chain, we need to embody a digital-first culture. A digital-first approach will require us to embrace new technological systems, data management, and sophisticated analytics. It also requires our teams to have vastly different skills and capabilities and gives us the opportunity to reimagine and simplify our processes. Please note that these will not be shock changes. They will occur over time. The key is that we start setting north stars now.

Reason #2: My moment of atonement

In *Trade Wars, Pandemics, and Chaos,* I made one grievous error: I fell into consultant groupthink. It's an easy mistake to make. In consulting, once an idea or topic emerges, it becomes a race of one-upmanship as everyone scrambles to establish their view on the topic du jour. Artificial intelligence, blockchain, ChatGPT, cryptocurrency, COVID-19, monkeypox, supply chain disruptions, inflation, the Russia–Ukraine war, and Industry 4.0 are just some of the thousands of topics that have emerged in the consulting profession. The problem is that consultants, analysts, and pundits treat the topics superficially and lack sufficient depth to be useful to practitioners. In the process, a collective groupthink takes hold in which nobody says anything that's too different from the others (see Chapter VII: *Hacking resilience: how quickly can your supply chain recover?* for a clear example of this). This is the mistake in *Trade Wars, Pandemics, and Chaos.* While completing the manuscript, I panicked and lobbed in some risk-related content that was neither useful nor differentiated. It wasn't wrong, just not helpful. Here is the excerpt in question:

As part of our new risk management approach, we need our category and commodity managers to be enabled to model different strategies in response to various risk situations. Part of their job descriptions should include doing forward-looking what-if analyses to test and create alternative outcomes in case of disruption. Then as the risks unfold, the proper strategy can be quickly deployed based on changing dynamics. The strategy should then be matched with clear roles and responsibilities in the response and finding the right balance between cost and risk mitigation/resilience. It is important to include accountability measures that continually track and evaluate the efficacy of strategy and actioning. Companies need to continually test the efficacy to ensure the proper allocation of resources in response to crises. Finally, automation should do the heavy lifting on low-risk events and should augment human intelligence augmentation on higher-risk events. Automation can also help run simulations and do the forward-looking scenario planning. This automation should take the form of anticipatory solutions that prompt users to think about what threats could happen and how to respond, and predictive solutions that predict threats that will likely happen.[1]

---

[1] Elouise Epstein. *Trade Wars, Pandemics, and Chaos: How digital procurement enables business success in a disordered world* (Chicago: Kearney, 2021).

Re-reading this makes me cringe because it doesn't get to a level of detail to be useful. I apologize to everyone who read that selection. I have written an updated risk chapter that I hope is practical and applicable to atone for that mistake.

Reason #3: My moment of philosophical musing

What is a supply chain? This question often keeps me up on sleepless nights. This seems like a simple question with a simple answer. And yet, ask 10 supply chain practitioners that question and you are likely to get 10 different answers. I talk to people from around the globe at companies from a few people to the largest enterprises. I'm always surprised at how many ways people describe supply chains. Add in the explosion of news stories, pundits, and technological innovation, and we have a profession whose essence is not clearly articulated.

A supply chain is one of those terms we seem to understand implicitly without a formal definition. The traditional description is "transforming raw materials into a product, and getting it to customers." AIMS UK logistics defines a supply chain as "[the] art and science of obtaining, producing, and distributing material and product in proper place and in proper quantities." Those definitions have formalized into the plan–source–make–deliver paradigm. Many curricula, training, and organizational structures are built around these towers. In recent years, quality and reverse logistics have been added.

The problem with this lack of clarity is that it increases the likelihood of mistakes. When one hand doesn't know what the other hand is doing (say planning and procurement or manufacturing and deliver) then critical information is likely to get dropped or misinterpreted. This is how we have ended up in a situation where most of today's supply chains run on Excel and email. Naturally, this creates a gigantic security risk and constrains our ability to meet customer and/or corporate objectives. I hope in some way this book can facilitate a discussion that helps us create a more precise answer, if for no other reason than that it will help me sleep at night. (See Figure 2: *The traditional supply chain towers* on page 8.)

Figure 2
The traditional supply chain towers

Plan	**Source**	**Make**	**Deliver**	**Reverse logistics**
— Predict/ manage demand — How much are we producing?	— Procure goods and services against demand	— Manufacturing the product or delivering the service	— Getting the product to the customer	— Returns and reclamation

Source: Kearney

How to read this book

The topic of supply chains is vast and seemingly overwhelming. Throughout the writing and editing of this book I have often wrestled with the unwieldy scope of this task. With that in mind I decided to use this book to address as many of the relevant topics as possible. As a result, I have structured this book like a graduate course whereby we'll dive deep into multiple subjects under a loose organizational umbrella. This allows for going both broad and deep into the material. Then we'll come together at the end to connect the dots. Feel free to read this book straight through or jump to the chapters that are most relevant and/or interesting.

Please note I have changed the names of individuals and companies to protect privacy and confidentiality unless I have express permission or the information is in the public sphere.

My argument

Today's supply chains are woefully insecure and lack sufficient resilience. Most supply chains were designed in a previous decade (if not century) at a time when enterprises controlled and ran most of their operations in-house. Yet today, a predominant number of supply chains have anywhere between 10,000 and 50,000 third-party entities that they interact with directly and tens of thousands further down the line (for example, a supplier's supplier). With this much reliance on third parties and associated complexity, we can no longer operate our supply chains in a business-as-usual manner. We must do something dramatically different. We must instead rebuild our supply chains from the ground up. To do that we must hack our supply chains to make them more secure and resilient and ready for the 21st century. For the purposes of this book, security is the act of protecting, and resilience is the ability to bounce back from disruption.

We need to embrace a culture of digital, increase our algorithmic and data literacy, and adopt a hacking mindset. In this context, hacking is looking critically at our systems (technical and process), tearing them down to their core component pieces, and reassembling them to meet the ever-evolving risk environment. According to security expert Bruce Schneier, "Hacking is a useful tool to understand a broad array of systems: how they fail, and how to make them more resilient." He goes on to note, "Hacking targets a system and turns it against itself without breaking it ... [it] subverts the intent of the system by subverting its rules and norms."[2]

Ultimately, this book is focused on how we get vastly better at managing third-party relationships to improve security, decrease risk, and ultimately create more resilience. All three will bring about value for any enterprise. A global cyberwar is underway right now, but most of us aren't aware of it. Enterprise supply chains are the most vulnerable to attack—if we can't even get toilet paper and cleaning supplies during a pandemic, what happens when our collective manufacturing systems are breached? Look no further than Russia's invasion of Ukraine, where both sides are deploying the most

---

[2] Schneier, Bruce. *A Hacker's Mind: How the Powerful Bend Society's Rules, and How to Bend them Back* (New York: W. W. Norton & Company, 2023), 8-10.

sophisticated cyberweapons against each other's infrastructure and suppliers. At the beginning of the war, one of Russia's weapons manufacturers was hacked, and schematics for Russian weapons were posted online. Hackers had exploited a vulnerability in the manufacturer's email server, which Microsoft had patched a year earlier.[3] The supplier had neglected to apply the patch. The cyberfighting is not limited to the two countries either, but many other entities have become involved, including organized crime, Anonymous (the hacktivist collective), and pretty much any hacker with an interest.

The problem is that the battlefield is not limited by physical boundaries in a digital world. The even bigger problem is that the sophisticated cyberweapons being deployed against nation-states have been and will continue to be used against nearly every enterprise business. Compared to nation-states, enterprise businesses are very soft targets. And if enterprises are soft, their suppliers and third parties are more vulnerable. This is just the beginning. We still have many physical security vulnerabilities in our supply chains. Typically, these occur in the space where the physical and digital world intersect. Most concerningly, people pose the greatest risk to our objective of secure and resilient supply chains.

We must take a series of important steps to protect against these threats. First is to make our entire teams (and especially leaders) highly proficient with digital capabilities. To be clear, one does not become digital by taking classes—being digital is not a trainable skill. Digital is a culture, a way of being. To truly become digital means having the right level of motivation and social incentive such that one decides to remove all obstacles to achieve their learning objective. We also need a flexible and extensible set of digital technologies at our fingertips that is built around secure data exchange with the proper third parties. This means moving away from legacy technical debt toward a more sophisticated, bespoke set of individual capabilities that are seamlessly integrated with one another.

[3] Seytonic. "Anonymous Hacks Russian Military." YouTube video. 7:41. February 27, 2023. https://www.youtube.com/watch?v=dwbDMnEraO0 (Accessed May 28, 2023).

Armed with a new culture and digital capability, we can begin to address building tomorrow's supply chains today. By making our supply chains more secure from the ground up, we will increase their resilience, efficiency, and social consciousness. There are many ways to look at the end-to-end supply chain. This is simply one. I'm not going to talk about Lean Six Sigma process improvement, optimizing the network of distribution/fulfillment centers, or lights out planning, which are all very valid topics (along with many more) and worthy of nonfiction books unto themselves (or perhaps fantasy books in terms of lights out planning). This book instead is about how a new approach to digital can reduce third-party supply chain risk—and help organizations build next-generation supply chains.

As a futurist, I am very skeptical of overhyped technology. Those familiar with my work know that I hate buzzwords, jargon, and erstwhile technological hype. I try to avoid the use of the terms AI, machine learning, blockchain, RPA, and the like. However, I will use them as a point of departure to explain and/or explore the underlying concepts. For example, I will talk about supply chain provenance in this book and naturally the question that comes up is, "What about blockchain?" I will answer this by explaining how we achieve provenance in a digital world, what can go wrong, and how blockchain or any other technology might be a good fit (and yes, blockchain is overhyped and has underdelivered). Too often, technology hype outpaces both the business need and the ability of people to understand it. In that chasm between capability, need, and understanding, people start to imagine that the technology represents a quick fix to an otherwise intractable problem—but the secret is that there are no quick fixes and no magic button. My previous book was about identifying the villains and holding them accountable. Fun though that was, that's not the goal here (though some folks may feel unduly poked at). I am working to move us all to a new place. Of course, in the process, old ways of working will fall by the wayside, and we will see pretty quickly that old technologies aren't sufficient (I'm looking at you, big ERP).

This doesn't mean we have to throw out the old, but we need to acknowledge that buying a new ERP system or consolidating 50 ERPs down to one is solving yesterday's complexity problem. To build the next-generation supply chains, we will have to get vastly more skilled at how we employ digital capabilities, correspondingly change our processes, and improve our capabilities.

The third-party landscape

Traditional business logic has stated that the customer is always right. Implicitly, this makes the customer the most important person in a business environment. I challenge this view by arguing that the third party is equally as important because if you can't get raw material for, manufacture, or deliver the product you have nothing to sell to the customer. Some of my colleagues contend that the employee is the most important entity in business because if you can't staff your enterprise, you can't sell anything to the fictional customer, much less produce and deliver it. Obviously all three of these entities are important. Tomorrow's enterprise success will be based on getting the balance right between customer, employee, and third party so that everyone wins. Historically, this equation has been out of balance to the detriment of the third party (and arguably the employee).

For the purposes of this book, third parties are any entity that interacts with an enterprise that is not a formal employee or the customer. This includes suppliers, partners (for example, healthcare providers, dealers, authorized representatives), government organizations (global/national/state/local), nongovernmental organizations (for example, the Red Cross, Amnesty International), transnational organizations (such as terrorist organizations, organized crime), loosely organized collectives of likeminded people working together (for example, the hacking collective Anonymous), and individuals such as evil billionaire villains. To build the next-generation supply chain, we need systems that properly exchange data and defend against all these entities. This is about putting these third parties front and center in the operations and in defense of our enterprises.

One of the least appreciated changes in our supply chains is exactly how much they rely on third parties. For example, consider the number of third parties required to produce, distribute, and deliver the COVID vaccine to my arm. At a minimum, there were the suppliers who provided the source materials that went into the vaccine, the logistics companies that transported the source materials, the manufacturer (Moderna) that produced the vaccine, the logistics companies that shipped it to the Walmart distribution centers (DCs), and the logistics companies that sent the vaccine from the DCs to the Walmart store. And this is a simple example that assumes that Moderna did their own production. Industries like consumer packaged goods (CPG) make extensive use of contract manufacturing and packaging suppliers to produce their goods before sending them to third-party logistics companies for warehousing and distribution. Not only is it complicated to visualize, but there are also some additional crucial problems. First is tracking data on all these systems. There is no universal data format, exchange mechanism, or even incentive to share data across all these third parties. Second, supply chain organizations are typically not built to handle end-to-end operations. Third, as should be obvious to even the most casual observer, there is tremendous opportunity for risk and disruption. Any nefarious character can break any supply chain—it doesn't matter what the industry is and it's not that hard. You simply need to vector through the third parties. Finally, the technology underpinning today's supply chains was designed and developed in the 1980s and 1990s and hasn't really evolved to confront the third-party way of operating, hence creating the data visibility and exchange problem. (See Figure 3: *Simplified vaccine supply chain* on page 14.)

Think about some of the recent high-profile data breaches such as Best Buy (the third party that provides chat services for the chain was breached and customer payment information was stolen in 2018[4]), Home Depot (hacked by using a supplier's name and password to infiltrate and steal 56 million customers' payment information, resulting in a $17.5 million settlement[5]), and Target (hackers stole a third party's credentials to access internal systems and steal 41 million customer payment records[6]). T-Mobile has been breached nine times since 2018.[7] These are all strikingly familiar in scope and impact— bad actors attack the third party to gain credentials, use the credentials to access the target network, install malware, steal payment information, and get rich. Then there was the SolarWinds attack, which exploited a weak third party in the software supply chain and embedded malware that was

[4] Jones, Charisse. "Best Buy Shoppers' Payment Information May Have Been Exposed in Data Breach." *USA Today*, April 6, 2018. https://www.usatoday.com/story/money/2018/04/06/best-buy-shoppers-payment-information-may-have-been-exposed-data-breach/493690002/ (Accessed May 11, 2023).
[5] Stempel, Jonathan. "Home Depot reaches $17.5 million settlement over 2014 data breach." Reuters, November 24, 2020. https://www.reuters.com/article/us-home-depot-cyber-settlement/home-depot-reaches-17-5-million-settlement-over-2014-data-breach-idUSKBN2842W5 (Accessed May 11, 2023).
[6] McCoy, Kevin. "Target to pay $18.5M for 2013 data breach that affected 41 million consumers." *USA Today*, May 23, 2017. https://www.usatoday.com/story/money/2017/05/23/target-pay-185m-2013-data-breach-affected-consumers/102063932/ (Accessed May 11, 2023).
[7] Goodin, Dan. "T-Mobile discloses second data breach of 2023, this one leaking account PINs and more." Ars Technica, May 11, 2023. https://arstechnica.com/information-technology/2023/05/t-mobile-discloses-2nd-data-breach-of-2023-this-one-leaking-account-pins-and-more/ (Accessed May 11, 2023).

Figure 3
Simplified vaccine supply chain

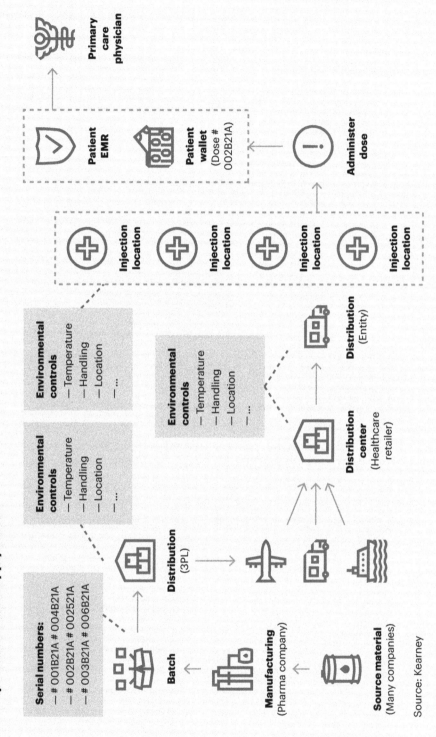

Source: Kearney

surreptitiously distributed further up the chain to the real targets (businesses and governments). These are all "supply chain attacks" in that they go for the weakest part of the supply chain—the third parties—and then use that to exploit further upstream. A supply chain attack is both pernicious and successful because the entire chain is built upon trust. All an attacker needs to do is find the weakest part, exploit it, and use the implied trust to work their way up the chain. So our jobs as supply chain managers, designers, and architects is to question the implied level of trust of third parties.

This extends to third parties that we don't even control such as nongovernmental organizations, certain political entities, or organized crime. We are at a once-in-a-generation moment as supply chain professionals. There is little doubt that governments will increasingly regulate supply chains, if not designate them national security interests (or perhaps even nationalize them). So this is our opportunity to define and build our future before it is done to us.

A new approach to supply chain design

I am arguing that we need to refine our understanding of how to do supply chain management data exchange to mitigate risk and increase efficiency. That means we need to establish intelligence across the entire supply chain and be nimble enough to pass that off to any and every third party that needs it. For example, consumer products will increasingly need to have provenance associated with them, which requires capturing every step of the source material, manufacturing, and distribution tied to every product.

We also need a new generation of fit-for-purpose digital tooling and architecture. We must disavow ourselves of the notion that ERP will lead us into the future, much less be relevant. And we need to increase the capability of everyone who does supply chain management.

In *Trade Wars, Pandemics, and Chaos*, I argued for the following skills:

— **Business athlete:** understanding the entirety of the business across multiple functions, not just the supply chain

— **Motivation:** finding the right levers to motivate employees to engage in learning

— **Digital:** wanting, embracing, and exploring technology

— **Analytically minded and data driven:** applying data to solve business problems

— **Emotional intelligence:** reading and reacting appropriately to other people's emotions

— **Creativity:** imagining and communicating beyond simple frameworks or playbooks

— **Problem life cycle management:** taking ownership of a problem from detection to resolution

— **Advanced communication:** communicating in multiple formats (written, visual, and so on)

— **Superb presentation skills:** telling a good story that is anchored in deep expertise

— **Executive presence:** learning to confidently interact with all manner of executives

— **Building respect/reputation:** strategically building and curating a personal brand

— **Synthesize for a multiplicity of audiences:** learning to present confidently to various audiences from the boardroom to the warehouse floor

For this book, I want to double down on these skills and discuss how we build them. And, to add a bit of urgency to this, since AI (namely generative AI) has entered the zeitgeist, "[i]t's not the AI that will take your job it's the person using AI that will take your job."[8] More broadly, we need to flex our digital skills and competencies. That means taking ownership and architecting systems that interoperate versus the traditional monolithic system.

---

[8] BCS, The Chartered Institute for IT. "AI isn't going to replace your job...someone using AI will!" YouTube video. 58:39. February 2023. https://www.youtube.com/watch?v=cPRCasuMDtA (Accessed May 28, 2023).

The transformation true-up[9]

The key to securing our supply chains, and ultimately making them more resilient, is to make the most of the vast amount of sophisticated digital technology available to us—whether it is AI, cloud infrastructure, robotics, sensors, you name it. Successfully employing these innovations will make supply chains (and enterprises) more efficient and effective, and perform better. Traditional logic has suggested that enterprises need to undergo massive digital transformations to embrace digital. Collectively, enterprises have spent billions upon billions of dollars on digital transformations. In the process, they've paid consulting companies, tech providers, and systems integrators to make them "digital." Recent studies have pegged the transformation success rate at less than 84 percent. I am very happy that everyone is attempting to digitally transform.[10] But it is galling that so much money is spent for such little impact. When I talk to people running supply chains (analysts to executives), they operate in a Digital 1.0 realm. Digital 1.0 uses email, spreadsheets, shared drives, PDF files, presentations, and offline notes.

If one is going to digitally transform, we should stop relying on these old methods. The adoption of all these tools dates back to the failures of ERP systems to transact in a flexible and extensible manner. But even beyond these tools, most employees I encounter don't possess adequate digital skills such as algorithmic fluency (understanding what different algorithms do), data conceptualization (visualizing the data needed against the data possessed), and tool competency (determining the best tool for the problem at hand). So we need to ask some questions to do our true-up. A true-up is an accounting term that means reconciling an estimated budgeted amount with the actual expenditure. We can use the same concept to assess the efficacy of digital transformations. If we spent $10/$25/$50 million on a digital transformation, was there a corresponding change in the level of digital ways of working and competencies? Did leaders redesign and even eliminate archaic processes?

---

[9] Credit to my Kearney colleague Matthew Totlis for coming up with this term.
[10] Block, Dr. Corrie. "12 Reasons Your Digital Transformation Will Fail." Forbes, Forbes Coaches Council, March 16, 2022. https://www.forbes.com/sites/forbescoachescouncil/2022/03/16/12-reasons-your-digital-transformation-will-fail/?sh=7d9ba76b1f1e. (Accessed May 11, 2023).

Are employees making use of all the powerful cloud technologies? Did the organization become data driven and create breakthrough intelligence insights? Sadly, the answer is almost always no.[11]

In their current form, transformations are a shield for perpetuating the status quo. They create a redoubt of inaction and excuses. If we do an accounting of what changed during a transformation, the answer is rarely anything significant. Sure, an organization may have changed a few ERP systems, added some new planning software and transactional systems, and provided some training. The goal is often standardization, which simplifies IT but ultimately isn't that useful. Digital is messy. But the messiness yields nimbleness. We see this in start-ups—everything is a fire drill/burning platform that drives excellence, learning through failure, and ultimately success.

Traditional enterprises need to stop looking longingly at digitally native companies Facebook, Amazon, Apple, Netflix, and Google (FAANG). Digital transformations are sold as if they will take 100-year-old companies and make them "data companies" and "digitally native," whereby everything is one click and you have access to perfect data and insights. Throw in some buzzwords and you have promises of grandeur, which have no prayer of being achieved. I have yet to see any traditional enterprise closely approximating or acting like FAANG. Perhaps we should stop deluding ourselves and set different goals for what it means to digitally transform. If we're going to undertake a digital transformation, let's start by evaluating the applicability of digital to the operation of our specific business and use that as a starting point.

[11] Garcia, Carolos. "J&J's Former Chief Procurement Officer on the Evolution of the Function," Heidrick & Struggles Leadership Podcast, episode 91, November 10, 2023, https://www.heidrick.com/en/insights/podcasts/e91_-jj-former-chief-procurement-officer-on-the-evolution-of-the-function (Accessed May 11, 2023).

Chapter II
The intelligence–tools–people paradigm

"The most insidious enemy in security is routine."

– Jerry Parr, US Secret Service Agent

Every time I see "framework" on a PowerPoint slide I visibly roll my eyes. It doesn't matter how good or bad the framework is or isn't. The trouble is that we have way too many frameworks, and many of them lack practical applicability or are too simplistic for the job at hand. The most popular is People, Process, Technology, but I've seen frameworks with up to eight strategic pillars. It's a problem that I loathe to admit I have contributed to over the years.

But wait, doesn't this chapter title indicate that another framework is forth-coming? My goal is to introduce three crucial concepts to improve our supply chains: intelligence, tools, and people. I'm not suggesting that these are the only strategic concepts needed in the future. I am simply drawing a laser focus on our requirement to develop new muscles for these capabilities and de-emphasize others. For example, process management is less relevant in a generative AI world where predefining hundreds or thousands of processes is anachronistic at best. I will let you as the reader (or other consultants) wrap them into a framework.

Rawhide down

On March 30, 1981—a high humidity, 65-degree cloudy day—newly elected US president Ronald Reagan walked out of the Washington, D.C. Hilton Hotel

VIP entrance.[12] As he approached the nearby limo, he turned to his left and waved at a group of approximately 30 reporters and press representatives. That is when six shots rang out in quick succession from a gun fired by John Hinckley Jr., who was hiding in the throng of reporters. In an instant, James Brady (Reagan's press secretary) was hit in the head and fell to the ground, while police officer Thomas Delahanty took a bullet in the back and fell to the ground. The third shot went sailing over Reagan's head. Upon hearing the shots, Secret Service agent Tim McCarthy did the most unnatural human act of whipping around and extending his body to protect the president—in the process, he took a bullet in the chest. The fifth shot hit the limousine door and the sixth shot hit the driveway. The next Secret Service agent, Jerry Parr, walking with the president, threw Reagan into the limo as shots fired. As they entered the car, the sixth bullet ricocheted off the limousine and hit Reagan under the left arm, puncturing a lung.[13] Secret Service agents rushed Reagan to the emergency room for surgery and the president emerged from the entire ordeal seemingly stronger than ever. There are many lessons to learn from this incident. However, there are an equal number of uncomfortable questions. According to historian Del Quentin Wilber in his book *Rawhide Down: The Near Assassination of Ronald Reagan*:

After the president's arrival at the Hilton, Hinckley had walked into the hotel's lobby and loitered there for a while, the gun still in his jacket pocket. Then he'd returned to the rope line and waited with the others in the crowd … Hinckley saw Reagan emerge from the VIP entrance. Unbelievably the president was completely out in the open and Reagan would pass right in front of him … Two police officers turned away toward Reagan; a S[ecret] S[ervice] agent looked at the ground. Nobody was paying any attention to him … He knew only that he would never get another chance as good as this one. He pulled the gun from his pocket.[14]

How did a random person just walk up to the press line, mere feet from the president, pull out a gun and nearly assassinate the leader of one of the

[12] Wunderground.com, https://www.wunderground.com/history/daily/us/dc/washington/KDCA/date/1981-3-30, accessed July 17, 2023.
[13] Video footage of the entire incident exists including Agent McCarthy spreading his arms and taking the bullet; however, the quality is not high enough for print.
[14] Del Quentin Wilber, *Rawhide Down: The Near Assassination of Ronald Reagan* (New York: Henry Holt and Co., 2011), 80.

world's two superpower countries? Also, why was nobody paying attention to activity in the crowd? The policemen were looking at Reagan—not the crowd—and the Secret Service agent was looking at the ground. Perhaps most concerningly, few of the agents or police officers, including the wounded ones, wore bulletproof vests either due to the weather or the fact that it was supposed to be a local "trip to the Hilton." (See Figure 4: *The Washington Hilton Layout* on page 22 and Figure 5: *The moment before the shooting* on page 23.)

How do we protect a president?

These days, the US Secret Service has a zero-fail mission statement when it comes to protecting the president. Failure to protect the president has catastrophic global consequences but also shines a spotlight on Secret Service failures, including the Reagan assassination attempt. Imagine a job where your job performance or lack thereof could influence the course of history. So the question is, how do we protect a president? I ask this question because it serves as a useful metaphor for supply chain risk management.

When it comes to protecting the president or other such dignitary, typically we think of bodyguards or Secret Service agents. That's largely because we see these protectors as the main line of defense in movies and on TV. In these representations, the protagonist is usually a physically fit bodyguard and that's not far from real life. However, humans are the most expensive and valuable assets. If the Secret Service agents are getting into the action, such as shooting their guns or acting as human shields, something has gone terribly wrong.

According to Jonathan Wackrow, former Secret Service agent, COO and global head of security for Teneo Risk, and a law enforcement analyst for CNN, to protect a president we must think in terms of concentric circles of protection:

— **Inner ring.** Direct human protection around the president.

— **Middle ring.** Physical security, limiting access through narrowing, police, metal detectors, decoys, alternative entrances (loading docks, covered entrances), HVAC protection.

Figure 4
The Washington Hilton layout

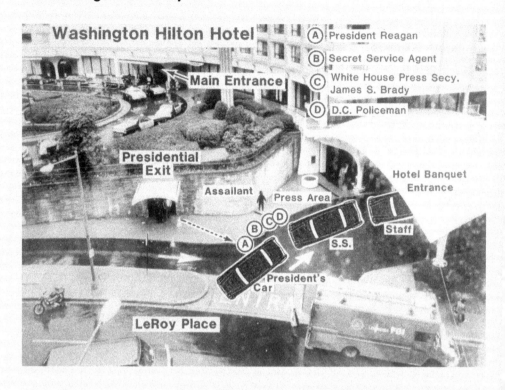

Figure 5
The moment before the shooting

Source: Courtesy Ronald Reagan Library

— **Outer ring.** Data and intelligence to identify potential threats through signal monitoring, situational analysis (updated daily), route design, and location selection.[15]

All of this to protect one person. However, it's a model that also applies to protecting supply chains, as I'll explain more in detail.

Security theater of the absurd

On March 13, 2020, in response to the rapidly unfolding coronavirus pandemic, the Transportation Security Administration (TSA) rescinded its 3.4 oz limit for hand sanitizer on planes. This change allowed travelers to bring up to 12 oz of hand sanitizer. The next day, Dan Kois, editor and writer at *Slate*, skewered the TSA (and much of American policy) for its capriciousness. The TSA's rule change showed just how arbitrary their 3.4 oz limit was and that risk to airline passengers had nothing to do with the amount of hand sanitizer allowed on planes. Kois was making a broader statement about how fear and punishment become tools to benefit power structures, primarily governments, instead of citizens.[16] In the process, Kois highlighted a larger and more concerning question about airline security. If I can bring 12 oz of hand sanitizer on a plane, a substance that is 99 percent alcohol, then why can I not bring 12 oz of shampoo, conditioner, or water? In fact, the deeper we look into the TSA operations, especially in comparison to the Secret Service protective methodology (intelligence, tools, and people), the more it becomes clear that airport security in America is for show.

As noted security expert and author Bruce Schneier points out, "Security is both a feeling and a reality. The propensity for security theater comes from the interplay between the public and its leaders. When people are scared, they need something done that will make them feel safe, even if it doesn't truly make them safer. Politicians naturally want to do something in response to crisis, even if that something doesn't make any sense." After the 9/11 terrorist attacks, US politicians federalized airport security. Before 9/11, airlines

[15] Wilber, *Rawhide Down*, 81.
[16] Kois, Dan. "TSA Now Allows You to Bring a Large Bottle of Hand Sanitizer in Your Carry-On." Slate, March 20, 2020. https://slate.com/news-and-politics/2020/03/coronavirus-tsa-liquid-purell-paid-leave-rules.html (Accessed May 11, 2023).

contracted their own private security services. Almost overnight, 45,000 federal employees took responsibility for American airport security.[17]

Government planners went to great lengths to create the stage on which the TSA performed its grand security ballet. TSA checkpoints enforce an invisible compliance by pushing travelers through a series of physical cues: lines snaking around stations, plexiglass dividers, podiums staffed by agents who physically look down on all who approach, passengers taking off shoes and belts, etc.[18] The charade continues with the officer uniforms, which are designed to mimic law enforcement attire. Transportation security officers (TSOs) are dressed in "properly fitting uniforms" that include royal blue shirts, heavy boots, brass badges, and shoulder boards denoting rank.[19] When a traveler approaches a TSA checkpoint the whole experience is meant to confer a look and feeling of law enforcement.

The problem with this choreography is that it's nothing more than a facade— it's security theater. TSOs have no law enforcement standing or training. They are not authorized to carry firearms, make arrests, or do anything other than to detain passengers and call law enforcement officers when issues arise.[20] In addition, the TSA does not prevent access. To get to the "secure" side of the airport, all one needs to do is to buy a ticket and not carry a prohibited item. There is nothing inherently secure about the area of the airport that's inside security other than there are no overt weapons. To be fair, the TSA has a scale problem in that they are trying to protect the many, whereas the Secret Service is protecting only the few. However, the techniques are vastly different. Prohibiting liquids, testing shoes, and other arbitrary measures are backward looking—they're attempting to prevent terrorist attacks that have already taken place. The best time to prevent a terrorist attack is during its planning process. By the time it gets to the execution phase

---

[17] Redden, Shawna Malvini. *101 Pat-Downs: An Undercover Look at Airport Security and the TSA.* (Virginia: Potomac Books, 2021), 15.
[18] Redden, *101 Pat-Downs*, 55.
[19] Redden, *101 Pat-Downs*, 55.
"Dress and Appearance Handbook." American Federation of Government Employees. https://www.afge.org/globalassets/documents/tsa/representation/dress-and-appearance---handbook.pdf (Accessed May 11, 2023).
"1100.73-2 TSO Dress and Appearance Responsibilities." Transportation Security Administration. https://www.tsa.gov/sites/default/files/foia-readingroom/1100.73-2_tso_dress_and_appearance_responsi-bilities.pdf (Accessed May 11, 2023).
[20] Redden, *101 Pat-Downs*, 50-51.

(at an airport) then it's mostly too late.[21] If the TSA operated more like the Secret Service, it would be focused on intelligence, tools, and training to prevent the next terrorist attack. Instead, they toil away daily, performing the theater of security and relying on luck and passengers' willingness to intervene. Case in point: on November 1, 2013, a man armed with a semi-automatic rifle walked into Terminal 3 at LAX and shot several TSOs, killing TSO Gerardo Hernandez. The gunman entered the "secure" section of the airport looking for people to murder. It wasn't until a Los Angeles Police Department tactical team showed up and confronted the gunman with lethal force did the threat become neutralized. TSOs, like the public, had to find cover and flee from the gunman as they are neither trained, equipped, nor expected to confront gunmen. By comparison, the White House is considered a "secure" location. This security has been tested in recent years by gunmen armed with semi-automatic rifles who have attempted unauthorized access. These bad actors experienced multiple levels of lethal and non-lethal force to prevent their unwarranted entry. Therefore to say that an airport has a "secure" area is slightly concerning.

The corporate corollary here is that risk monitoring tools are performing the same role as TSA security. To say that a corporation has a risk management program simply because they have a risk monitoring tool is like saying there's a "secure area" in US airports. This leads to a philosophical problem in the TSA's approach: the agency focuses on "dangerous items" rather than "dangerous people or plots." Schneier goes on to advocate that airport security should be focused on intelligence agencies outside the airport. If government agencies and law enforcement are going to spy on their citizens, they might as well put that data to good use. With a greater focus on intelligence *before* a traveler gets to the airport, we can stop performing security theater and go back to the vastly more efficient airport security of pre-9/11 levels.[22]

The TSA suffers from another problem that corporate leaders should note: people performance. Given that TSOs are simply low-value commodity actors

---

[21] Schneier, Bruce. "Beyond Security Theater." *Schneier on Security.*
https://www.schneier.com/essays/archives/2009/11/beyond_security_thea.html (Accessed May 11, 2023).
[22] Schneier, Bruce. "Reassessing Airport Security." *Schneier on Security.*
https://www.schneier.com/blog/archives/2015/06/reassessing_air.html (Accessed May 28, 2023).

in a play, their management treats them as such. TSO compensation ranks as one of the lowest in the US government; add that they spend their first two years on probation and are constantly being monitored, tested, and surveilled. As one TSO put it, "Everyone [is] always afraid of making a mistake and getting fired."[23] It's not exactly the best culture. Correspondingly, the TSA also ranks bottom in job satisfaction among US government agencies.

To summarize, in the 20-plus years since the TSA's creation, the US has spent nearly $150 billion, with a severe return on investment disparity. As easy as it is to highlight the TSA's ongoing failures, mismanagement, and colossal waste of money, this is a clarion call for corporations to change their approach and stop putting on their own theatrical productions. Instead, we need a risk strategy based in reality which, like the Secret Service, employs intelligence, tools, and people in a pragmatic way.

[23] Becker, Scott. *TSA Baggage: An Inside Look at the Good, the Bad, and the Ugly at America's Airports* (Vermont: Skyhorse, 2017).

Chapter III
Intelligence: data underpins everything

"Perfect is the enemy of good."

– Voltaire

"If you come to the end of your transformation and your data isn't clean, you haven't transformed."

– Elouise Epstein

As we learned from the US Secret Service, the key is to use intelligence to mitigate risk before it even materializes. However, to create intelligence we need good, actionable data. This can be a challenge in a world that is creating vast amounts of data noise. Finding ways to cut through the noise and make data relevant can facilitate improved understanding and situational aware-ness. My goal here is to illustrate a very simple way to track and govern data and its role in controlling algorithms. This is the same skill buildup that we need to do with third-party data. (See Figure 6: *Elouise's tracking spreadsheet* on page 30.)

Figure 6
Elouise's tracking spreadsheet

Date	Day of the week	Daily reading	Daily writing	Daily video	Crossword	Stretching	Self care
9/1/2022	Thursday	Yes	Yes	Yes	Yes	No	Yes
9/2/2022	Friday	Yes	Yes	Yes	Yes	Yes	Yes
9/3/2022	Saturday	No	No	Yes	Yes	Yes	Yes
9/4/2022	Sunday	Yes	Yes	Yes	Yes	Yes	Yes
9/5/2022	Monday	Yes	No	Yes	Yes	Yes	Yes
9/6/2022	Tuesday	No	No	Yes	Yes	Yes	Yes
9/7/2022	Wednesday	No	No	Yes	Yes	Yes	No
9/8/2022	Thursday	No	No	Yes	Yes	Yes	Yes
9/9/2022	Friday	No	No	Yes	Yes	Yes	Yes
9/10/2022	Saturday	Yes	Yes	Yes	Yes	Yes	Yes
9/11/2022	Sunday	No	Yes	Yes	Yes	Yes	No
9/12/2022	Monday	No	No	Yes	Yes	Yes	Yes
9/13/2022	Tuesday	No	No	Yes	No	Yes	No
9/14/2022	Wedneday	No	No	Yes	Yes	Yes	No
9/15/2022	Thursday	No	No	No	Yes	Yes	Yes
9/16/2022	Friday	No	No	No	No	No	No
9/17/2022	Saturday	No	Yes	No	Yes	Yes	Yes
9/18/2022	Sunday	No	No	No	No	No	No
9/19/2022	Monday	No	No	No	No	No	No
9/20/2022	Tuesday	No	No	No	No	No	No
9/21/2022	Wednesday	No	No	No	No	No	No
9/22/2022	Thursday	No	No	No	No	No	No
9/23/2022	Friday	No	Yes	No	Yes	Yes	Yes
9/24/2022	Saturday	No	No	Yes	Yes	No	Yes
9/25/2022	Sunday	No	No	No	No	No	No
9/26/2022	Monday	No	No	Yes	Yes	Yes	Yes
9/27/2022	Tuesday	No	No	No	No	No	No
9/28/2022	Wednesday	No	No	Yes	Yes	No	No
9/29/2022	Thursday	No	No	Yes	Yes	Yes	Yes
9/30/2022	Friday	No	No	No	No	No	No
10/1/2022	Saturday	Yes	Yes	Yes	Yes	No	Yes

Source: Elouise Epstein

The data value chain

I loathe it when consultants create arbitrary frameworks to convey simple concepts. However, when it comes to data and analytics, it is useful to illustrate the journey from data to intelligence. This provides a way to understand the process and to point out the differences between data and intelligence. (See Figure 7: *The data value chain*.)

What is data?

It seems like every day I read about how important data is and how we need to have a "data-driven culture" and "intertwine data" into the business. That all sounds great on a PowerPoint slide, but it's quintessential consultant jargon, which I too am guilty of perpetuating. We need to move past these platitudes. Instead of talking about being "data driven," we need to say: Where do I get the data I need? How do I make it usable? And most importantly, what can I do

Figure 7
The data value chain

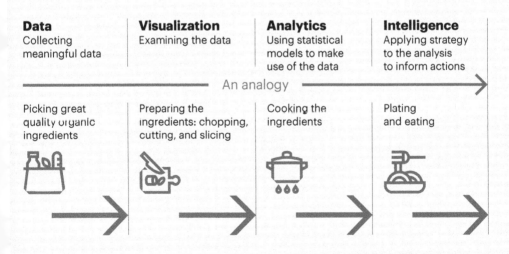

Source: Kearney

with it? In our future supply chain design, the crucial question is: How do we acquire, maintain, and refresh data from all the third parties we interact with?

It's also deeply important that we understand what we mean when we talk about data. Is it financial numbers on a spreadsheet? Is it an Excel file extracted from a system? Is it the data sitting in an ERP system? The answer is it's all of that and much more. Social sciences professor, researcher, and author Rob Kitchin defines data as "the raw material produced by abstracting the world into categories, measures, and other representational forms—numbers, characters, symbols, images, sounds, electromagnetic waves, bits—that continue the building blocks from which information and knowledge are created."[24] In short, everything is data. Whatever room you're in, there is data surrounding you. You are walking data, and every digital device you have—especially your phone—is a data beacon, leaving digital traces everywhere you go. If, by chance, you're reading this on a plane or train (or on your next plane or train trip, take a moment and look around), what data do you see?

— How many people are there?

— What is the gender breakdown?

— Can you make assumptions about age?

— What digital devices do you see? Can you see what people are doing on their devices?

— How are people dressed and are there any commonalities such as number of sweaters, jackets, hats, earrings, and so on?

— How many people are visibly sick? (Let's hope you aren't sitting next to them.)

— Is anybody reading a physical book?

[24] Kitchin, Rob. *The Data Revolution: Big Data, Open Data, Data Infrastructures & Their Consequences.* (Los Angeles: Sage Publications Ltd, 2014), Chapter 1: Conceptualizing Data.

— Are there any markers that suggest people's origin or destination?

— How many people are carrying single-use plastic?

If you formally collected this data, what could you do with it? If I asked you to sell a piece of software to these people, who would you start with and why? What about risk—do you see any overt risks? Who on the trip is using the most carbon?

Visualization: the limitations of dashboards

A client recently told me they had 430,000 contracts stored in their contract management system. I applauded the fact that they had that many documents and they knew where they were located. A fair number of my clients don't have a handle on where their contracts are located. Then I waited for an awkward amount of time for the client to expound on what juicy insights they had found from all those contracts. When it was clear that no more information would be forthcoming, I moved on. Somewhere my client has a dashboard counting all the contracts and showing basic metadata. This is a good example of visualizing data. Visualizations allow me to see what data I have, but they do nothing to tell me how that data influences my operations or what I could be doing differently. And to get the data out of a dashboard to influence business decisions takes multiple steps.

What I wanted this person to do was give me information about what's in those contracts. How many are active, how many different suppliers, what are the contract clause variations, and how many are up for renewal—the basics. One need not be a data scientist or understand advanced math to get these answers. You can be like me and have an unending curiosity for exploring data. My client was simply doing what was required—collecting and storing documents. That is not digital. To be digital would be to rip through those documents with an insatiable thirst to know what lies within (I still want to know what's in them). It would be looking at those documents and transforming them into something relevant. That data tells a whole story about my client's suppliers and ways of working. The fact that I know there are 430,000 documents sitting alone in a contract management system just begging to be explored is something I can't let go. To get at this information, we need to use more sophisticated analytical modeling.

Analytics: but what if I'm terrible at math?

Whenever I turn around, someone tells me we need to do "real-time analytics" or some equivalent. I barely passed high school algebra and somehow stumbled through college algebra, where I put probability theory to the test by guessing most of my answers. Then I studied history in graduate school, where I was able to sidestep statistics by studying two foreign languages (Spanish and German). But I digress; how is it I can do the "analytics" that everyone keeps telling me about when I don't know the difference between a sine and a quadratic equation?[25]

Interestingly and somewhat relatedly, I have become fascinated with the Bayesian statistical theory (BST), which is a theory for determining probability based on prior knowledge. It is used in all manner of practical applications, including artificial intelligence, bioinformatics, courtrooms, and war. It was a war example where the theory caught my attention. As someone who studies war extensively, I was immediately intrigued to learn that BST has a long and storied series of applications in modern war. Pioneering mathematical genius Alan Turing used BST to reduce the number of probabilities while cracking the German Enigma encryption machine. This was utterly compelling and has led me down many rabbit holes researching how Turing cracked the code. Post WWII, the US military has used BST to find a missing nuclear submarine and a lost nuclear bomb off the coast of Spain, and to help in coast guard search and rescue operations. As soon as I found a thread of personal interest, I became much more comfortable swimming in the mathematics that normally eludes me.[26]

Fortunately, tools now will do sophisticated analytics without me having to type a formula. Most of the analytics tools on the market can walk a user

---

[25] Yes, I look up common math equations randomly. I at least know that sines are part of geometry and quadratic equations are part of algebra, but that's about the sum total of what I know.
[26] McGrayne, Sharon Bertsch. *The Theory That Would Not Die: How Bayes' Rule Cracked the Enigma Code, Hunted Down Russian Submarines, & Emerged Triumphant from Two Centuries of Controversy.* (New Haven: Yale University Press, 2011). Making it personal is one of the key learning principles we will cover in Chapter X.

through the creation and application of analytical models. All you have to do is upload your data and explore the available analyses. There are even features in these tools that will allow surface insights you didn't even know to ask of your data.

Going back to the 430,000 contracts, we could use these same analytical tools to interrogate the contents. We could surface variations in payment terms, risk clauses, or simply cancelation terms. We can analyze the time spent on contract creation and look for ways to reduce inefficiencies. We could also combine spend and performance data to analyze how the suppliers we pay the most are performing and correlate that to commonalities or differences in their contracts.

Turning data into intelligence

In the summer of 2022, I took four weeks off to write this book. Two weeks into my writing sequestration, I realized I was spending more time watching YouTube video clips and bingeing on Netflix instead of writing. So I decided to start with a simple experiment. I would try to read for 30 minutes, write for 30 minutes, and watch YouTube clips related to the book for 30 minutes.[27] I tracked this as a way of keeping myself accountable and to measure my progress. I am very driven by my own individual performance. I am constantly pushing myself beyond my limits, whether it's having an absurd travel schedule, doing 16 Zoom calls in a day, or writing five books in 10 years (this is book three).

It wasn't long before I realized that I was interested in tracking other elements of my life, so I added a fourth dimension—self-care. The goal was to see if I was doing something each day to look after myself. But self-care turned out to be highly variable. One day it was watching the animated series *Harley Quinn* and the next it was taking a nap. I added two fields, one to track whether I did self-care, and the other to describe what I did if I met the objective.

Over time I started to become very curious about what else I could be tracking. I had five fields (date, writing, reading, video, self-care, self-care

[27] For a list of books and videos I consumed please go to https://www.drelouise.com/post/how-to-hack-your-supply-chain.

description). But I also have an Apple watch and I was trying to close the three rings (move, exercise, and stand) each day as well. Here was a device that was generating data about my physical performance and inducing different behavior. I was (and am) fixated on achieving the daily/weekly/monthly goals. This got me thinking about what would happen if I extended my data model with data from my Apple watch. One would think that all you'd have to do is click a button on the watch and it would send an export of your watch data to a spreadsheet that could be imported. Not the case.

I went down an obsessive path to figure out how to export data from my watch, which requires using the health app on my iPhone. Unfortunately, the export came out not in a CSV file, but XML. So I had to find an app to do XML-to-CSV exports (HealthExport), which converted the health data to a CSV file that I could incorporate into my spreadsheet. Once I managed to import the data, I looked to see how I could streamline and automate this process.

This is what it means to be digital. Digital is messy. When tools don't work, you need to poke, prod, and experiment to figure out how to get the data and/or functionality you want. Not that the individual choices matter too much, but these are the elements of data governance that have to be reconciled and these are the trade-offs and elements that every leader has to understand. This is what it means to get your hands dirty with data. For the non-quants, this is a good way to enter the world of data.

This whole exercise provides a useful anecdote on the data value chain. I started by capturing the data, then I visualized it so I could see what was happening. I analyzed the trends to inform what improvements I could or should make. However, it was only when I used these insights to create strategy that changed my behavior that the data became intelligence.

Needlessly overcomplicating third-party data governance

My intelligence example above brought forth a series of data governance problems. If data is an everyone *opportunity,* then data governance is an everyone *responsibility.* For the data tracking example above, here are some of the questions I had to wrestle with:

— What do I do if I write for 25 minutes and not 30? (If I go over 27 minutes I round up, otherwise I don't count the effort.)

— What if I forget to set my timer while reading? (For reading, I will equate a one-page read to one minute of reading and I don't have a measure for writing.)

— What do I do if I go a couple of days without inputting the data and can't remember if I did something? (My default is to assign "No" across the board.)

At a certain point I needed to make clear decisions so that I could make effective use of the data. This was a hard process and to this day I find myself debating whether I need to revisit the rules.

Now imagine supplier records. Think about all the various data elements for one company: legal name, headquarters address, subsidiaries, parent company, ownership structure, leadership, banking information, satellite offices, plant locations, warehouses, and so on. This doesn't include any risk or ESG data. We can quickly have hundreds, if not thousands, of fields for a single supplier. How do we govern this data?

This is where leaders need to lead and get their hands dirty. Leaving data governance to random teams of volunteers—or worse, middle managers—will ensure the failure of data governance. Except in rare cases, middle managers will overly complicate the governance process by trying to allow for every possible permutation. Here activity outweighs productivity. In an enterprise with many ERPs, getting data governance correct is a red herring. You need to get it good enough instead of perfect. This means making clear and concise decisions and moving on. For example, in my question above about writing 25 minutes versus 30 minutes, I just need to choose. I have seen the corporate world take a simple decision like that and create the most convoluted solution. To witness spectacular complexity and failure of data governance, simply look at any company's benefits tracking.

Our inability to effectively measure and track benefits is one of the great embarrassments of our profession. There's little benefit in having the perfect solution.

Part of operating in a digital mindset is to work as if everything is continually evolving versus do-it-once-and-change-it-never. Today's data governance decisions should be continually revisited, improved, and changed. In my example above, I started with three simple measures and gradually I extended my data model. Each time I did this, it brought new governance questions and choices. This did not derail my progress or even slow it down. Just like citing any research, I created data definitions, what fields I am tracking, where the data is coming from, and of course the answers to the questions that come up. There is no reason not to document the provenance of our data so people can understand how and what choices were made. It's no different than a research paper or a business case. This is how we start to build good data hygiene practices. When we make data interesting and relevant to everyone is when we start to solve some of these problems.

Thus, we need to quit holding out for a hero or a magic button.

Someone else is not going to fix it and no tool will miraculously fix our bad data. If the entire business does not embrace governance, then we will have perpetually bad data. We all need to roll up our sleeves, embrace the pain, and get to work. It's like making a meal: if everyone participates in preparing, cooking, and eating it, then everyone had better participate in the cleanup. Data governance is *hard*. (See sidebar: *Elouise's data for tracking* on page 39.)

Hacking intelligence: five takeaways

— Use intelligence to mitigate risk before it materializes.

— Digital is messy; embrace it.

— Data governance is an everyone opportunity.

— Understand the data value chain.

— Overcome your fears of not understanding analytics.

Elouise's data for tracking

I created my simple tracking sheet in Airtable, a fancy online spreadsheet that automatically brings the different columns to life with imagery and extensive use of color. This made the data readily accessible and engaging to me— instantly appealing, as I don't respond well to numbers on spreadsheets (but anybody can do the same exercise in Excel or any other spreadsheet software). The goal was to make the data easy to track. Additionally, for ease of use my entries are Yes or No; however, you quickly realize that to do any useful analysis the Yeses and Nos have to be converted into 1s and 0s. I choose to use the Yes/No paradigm because it's more pleasing to me and I'm happy to do the conversion as a later activity. Again, these are the types of trade-offs and decisions that leaders must stick their nose into, otherwise data governance teams can quickly find themselves creating overcomplicated workaround rules that don't help.

Chapter IV
Tools: we are in a post-ERP world; we just haven't accepted it yet

"We are waiting for big ERP."

– CPG company

"It's a train wreck ... they [each business unit] are using different legacy (big ERP) systems ... systems and platforms are not integrated. People need to manually extract and input data, resulting in data accuracy issues."

– Medical devices company

When it comes to protecting the president, the tools employed by the US Secret Service provide the active protection mechanism. But these tools only work if they are the right tools for the job and the tools are being used. We wouldn't want the president to ride in an unarmored vehicle. Similarly, those charged with protecting the president should have personal protective tools. Unfortunately, as evidenced during the Reagan assassination attempt, oftentimes we have the tools but we fail to use them. This brings us to the current state of supply chain systems, which rely almost exclusively on the biggest, most expensive tool around—the ERP. This is the equivalent of driving the president in an unarmored car protected by Secret Service agents with no body armor.

We have fit-for-purpose systems for sales (customers) and human resources (employees). So why do we not have one for third parties? There is little question that we need a singular customer record. There is no question that we need a singular record for employees. So how do we not have a singular record for third parties? We have requisition-to-pay systems that are focused on paying third parties. We have myriad ERP systems that manage material planning and execution and, in some cases, pay third parties. We severely lack a singular system that manages all the information surrounding a third party. This would include all the information about the supplier (locations, contacts, banking), data exchange (demand forecasts, orders, changes), and intelligence (risk, ESG, supply market).

Right now, the best we have is a record of when and where payment occurred and to whom. This is limiting because it assumes every third party will transact directly. It also puts the focus on the transaction and not the third-party entity. This forces us to look at third-party information management and data exchange backward, which is the result of legacy supply chain system development. The near-monopolistic grip that the few big ERP providers wield chokes innovation and ensures companies stay focused on solving yesterday's problems instead of building for tomorrow's needs.

What if we could start over? What if we could build a new supply chain system from scratch? What would a supply chain system built around data exchange with third parties look like? What if we didn't have to deal with legacy technical debt, 1990s architecture, and pre-information era (and even the emerging AI era) designs? Without these constraints, we could build a fit-for-purpose supply chain architecture and ecosystem of tools with third parties at the center. This ecosystem would enable the creation of crucial intelligence, the desperately needed third-party data exchange, and the intelligence to empower our people to meet the challenges of operating a 21st century supply chain.

The digital tipping point

When it comes to supply chain management systems, I argue that we have hit the tipping point at which we can no longer solely buy off-the-shelf software. First, today's business environment is vastly different and infinitely more complicated than when big ERP debuted 30 or 40 years ago. Consider the continual acquisition, divestiture, and separation of big enterprises. Unsurprisingly, 97 percent of Apple's supply chain runs through third parties.[28] Amazon, quaintly dubbed "The Everything Store," is continually branching out into new business endeavors to make its operations simultaneously more complicated, efficient, and cost-effective. The company is running a 21st century supply chain design against competitors rooted in 20th century designs. In the process, they are continually putting competitive pressure on traditional stores such as Walmart, Target, Best Buy, and logistics companies like FedEx and DHL.

Amazon has constructed many of its systems around a custom-built digital backbone. The wildly successful Amazon Web Services (AWS), originally built to power The Everything Store, grew from $3 billion in revenue in 2013 to more than $62 billion in 2021.[29] Its platform as a service (PaaS) allows for dynamic (elastic in Amazon nomenclature) scaling of infrastructure and ready access to the latest in analytics, machine learning, AI, and other such innovations, powering the most complicated supply chain in the world. More importantly, this has put Amazon and AWS at the forefront of the most revolutionary supply chain innovations in robotics (Kiva acquisition, RoboMaker simulation), IoT data collection and management (IoT Core), and even satellite connectivity (Amazon Ground Station). This is on top of acquiring their own air fleets and container ships. In late 2022, AWS announced a new supply chain offering, which aims to push supply chain design into vastly new realms. By comparison, simply buying an ERP system to run operations for a multinational enterprise in the era of disruptions seems anachronistic at best and derelict at worst. To amplify this point, most global enterprises carry significant technical debt in the way of tens or even hundreds of disparate ERP systems. These systems will never be integrated and attempting to integrate them into a single instance is a fool's errand. ERP consolidation is the biggest game of whack-a-mole ever. Most of these consolidation initiatives last six to eight years and never reach their

[28] Gupta, Poornima. "Apple reveals supply chain, details conditions." Reuters, Business News, January 13, 2012. https://www.reuters.com/article/uk-apple-suppliers-apple-reveals-supply-chain-details-conditions-idUKTRE80C1KV20120113. (Accessed May 11, 2023).
[29] Vailshery, Lionel Sujay. "Development of Amazon Web Services Revenue." Statista. February 27, 2023. https://www.statista.com/statistics/233725/development-of-amazon-web-services-revenue/ (Accessed May 11, 2023).

destinations. Companies spend billions of dollars with systems integrators and big ERP providers to consolidate these ERP systems. Most efforts never bear the promised fruit and some end in spectacular failures and lawsuits. Consider the following very public ERP failures:

— National Grid (the New York utility company) attempted to replace one big ERP provider with another big ERP provider for internal financial systems. The budget estimate was almost $400 million. A series of flaws, including dispersing wrong payments, resulted in the need to bring on almost 1,000 contractors to fix both the system and business problems associated with this failure. The total cost of the project came in at almost $1 billion.[30]

— German retailer Lidl suffered a complete failure of its big ERP platform and had to write off €500 million. The worst part is they had to revert to their previous system.[31]

— DHL (the global logistics provider) had to write off €338 million and revert to their legacy system when their big ERP failed.[32]

There are two sides to every story and lots of blame to go around. Big ERP likes to point at the systems integrators. The systems integrators blame big ERP. And big ERP, the systems integrators, and the consultants blame the client.

These high-profile stories of failure are not one-offs. There are many lawsuits that get settled out of court. And, from my own experience, nearly every large enterprise I work with has a similar story. This is an open secret in the supply chain profession. Very few people would disagree with these statements about big ERP's inadequacies; the problem is, what's the alternative? Interestingly, there are even big ERP expert witnesses for hire that will "write expert opinions and/or testify in over a dozen [big ERP] lawsuits."[33]

[30] Kim, Eugene. "National Grid's SAP Upgrade Will Cost Over $1 Billion." Business Insider, October 6, 2014. https://www.businessinsider.com/national-grid-sap-1-billion-upgrade-cost-2014-10 (Accessed May 11, 2023).
[31] Kimberling, Eric. "Lessons from an SAP Failure at Lidl." Third Stage Consulting, August 5, 2018. https://www.thirdstage-consulting.com/lessons-from-an-sap-failure-at-lidl/ (Accessed May 11, 2023).
[32] Noyes, Katherine. "SAP: Don't blame us for DHL's logistics woes." Computerworld, November 17, 2015. https://www.computerworld.com/article/3010496/sap-dont-blame-us-for-dhls-logistics-woes.html (Accessed May 11, 2023).
[33] Kimberling, Eric. "My Life as an SAP Expert Witness," July 6, 2018. https://www.thirdstage-consulting.com/my-life-as-an-sap-expert-witness/ (Accessed May 11, 2023).

Regardless of why this keeps happening, if we're looking at write-offs of $500 million, perhaps we should be taking a closer look at what big ERP is actually giving us. If there is a market for expert witnesses to testify in ERP failures, then it's at least worth asking if there is a better way.

History of the ERP

ERP systems are, in a word, old. They trace their origins to the inventory control systems from the 1960s. The next major evolution came in the 1980s with material requirements planning (MRP) software, which was used to coordinate specifications, sourcing materials, manufacturing, and product delivery. In the 1990s, the ERP became the unifying integrator of marketing, finance, and operations into a single integrated platform. Those days seem so quaint compared to the massive chaos and complexity that confronts us today. Of course, this means that today's complicated supply chains run on software that was innovative in the 1990s. As I wrote in *Trade Wars, Pandemics, and Chaos:*

Today, supply chains run on software that was designed in the late 1990s. ERPs were new and innovative before 2000—and they have yet to measurably change. Of course, business has changed dramatically in that time. Large enterprises, especially those that grew through acquisition, are far more complex than they used to be. Consumers expect more, businesses need to operate more efficiently, there's greater government regulation, increased competition (where your suppliers often become your competitors), and general supply disruptions (war, tariffs, natural disasters, pandemics, and the like).

(See Figure 8: *Today's broken supply chain systems* on page 46.)

Figure 8

Today's broken supply chain systems

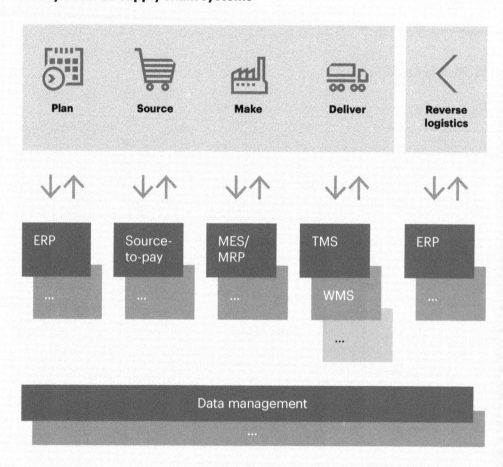

Source: Kearney

Notes: ERP is enterprise resource planning. MES/MRP is manufacturing execution system/material requirements planning. TMS is transportation management systems. WMS is warehouse management systems.

As supply chain leaders, designers, and professionals, we need a whole new generation of tools that take advantage of the latest technology developments, create end-to-end intelligence, empower human intelligence, and are built around integrations and interactions with third parties.[34] It's not hard to imagine that the multimillion (tens of millions) big ERP software deals and associated systems implementations/upgrades will steadily decline. To be clear, this is not to say we need to rip-and-replace existing ERP systems, but rather to acknowledge that the future of supply chain systems design needs to be more fluid and nimbler and not solely dependent on a singular, one-size-fits-all big ERP provider.

This is the crux of what it means to be digital. Given the uniqueness of how businesses operate today and the disruptions they face, future solutions will require some off-the-shelf components and bespoke applications while carrying over legacy technical debt loads. More specifically, enterprises will need to build and maintain some key parts of their supply chain infrastructure.

The next-generation supply chain platform

The reality is that billions upon billions have been invested in ERP systems, and many more hundreds of millions will be allocated in the upcoming years. This is a slow-moving ship that will take a long time to turn. However, the ubiquity of ERP systems does not mean that they are in fact solving the problem they claim to fix. More importantly, ERP systems are not useful for the future supply chain. So, ERPs will likely remain, but they will increasingly be sublimated to being a transactional system of record. Of course, this will leave some difficult questions about ROI and failed business cases. And every big ERP investment today increases the technical debt ceiling.

The next-generation supply chain platform will be borderless, built to facilitate ubiquitous data transfer from every possible third party that needs to consume or share data with our supply chain systems. There are five core components to designing the next-generation supply chain platform (NGP): cloud infrastructure, data foundation, functional capabilities (plan/source/

[34] Thomson, Piper. "The Complete History of ERP: Its Rise to a Powerful Solution," January 23, 2020. https://www.g2.com/articles/history-of-erp (Accessed May 11, 2023).

make/deliver/reverse logistics), intelligence, and user experience and orchestration. (See Figure 9: *A new supply chain architecture* on page 49.)

Each of these foundational components is designed for multilateral enterprise data exchange. First and foremost, the NGP will be built upon a cloud infrastructure. This is now Amazon Web Services, Microsoft Azure, or Google Cloud Platform. However, over time this may change as new providers hit the market or companies create their own cloud. Regardless of which one, the cloud infrastructure needs to have vast and ever-growing capabilities that stay current with the latest infrastructure (virtual machines, networking, compute, storage, backups, and so on), the latest AI/analytics libraries, and extended technology capabilities (robotics, digital ledger, IoT, satellites, and so on). The data foundation is also essential; this includes all data management and connections to internal and external data sources along with the requisite data governance, ESG, and risk enrichments.

We must also account for the foundational supply chain capabilities (for example, plan, source, make, deliver, reverse logistics). Short term, this is where legacy ERP systems will continue to serve a role as transactional systems of record, but over time these will be replaced by bespoke solutions that simplify transactions. Next is the intelligence layer. This is where we will build our supply chain control tower—an amalgamation of data from all internal supply chain functional areas (plan, source, make, deliver, reverse logistics) and external third parties to holistically model, operate, and respond to supply chain needs, opportunities, and disruptions. The last component will be the user experience and process orchestration layer. This is where we provide a singular, personal-ized user experience to every user and role that interacts with the system. Historically, users had to be grouped into predefined, preprogrammed groups. We can now use intelligence to give every user a custom experience based on who they are and what they do in the system. Closely tied with the user experience is process orchestration. Think of process orchestration as putting intelligent guardrails of what users can or cannot do in the system. These guardrails will be dynamic and make use of machine intelligence that interprets user intent, asks clarifying questions, and guides different outcomes versus hard prevention rules. Hard-coded prevention rules frustrate users. Process orchestration makes extensive use of no- or low-code solutions. (See sidebar: *The end of process mapping* on page 50.)

Figure 9

A new supply chain architecture

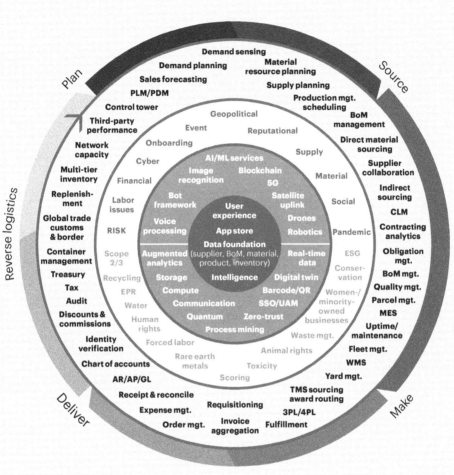

Source: Kearney

Notes: BoM is bill of materials. CLM is contract life cycle management. MES is manufacturing execution system. WMS is warehouse management system. TMS is transportation management system. AR/AP/GL is accounts receivable/accounts payable/general ledger. PLM/PDM is product life cycle management/product data management. ESG is environmental, social, governance. EPR is environmental producer responsibility. AI/ML is artificial intelligence/machine learning. SSO/UAM is single sign-on/universal access management. NGO is nongovernmental organization. BPO is business process outsourcing.

The end of process mapping

One very important digital innovation is the emergence of workflow orchestration systems. These tools interface and exchange data with downstream systems to provide a consistent user experience. The tools are no or low code, which means any business user can define a workflow through a very simple drag-and-drop interface without programming skills. For example, at the beginning of the week we could create a new workflow for suppliers to self-service check on invoice statuses. Then on Tuesday we could create a new workflow for contractors to requisition software licenses. Wednesday we could create a workflow to pipe crude oil commodity pricing data and the pricing rates from our contract repository to our commodity manager for evaluation.

These workflow orchestration tools stitch together the vast complexity of systems into a single easy-to-operate interface for internal or external users accessing our systems. This can include multi-application task management, data collection, communication streams, and almost any other imaginable use case. Historically this level of data collaboration was only possible through complicated ERP integration, but this was self-defeating because it made maintenance, system updates, and upgrades more complicated and in some cases impossible. With these new orchestration tools, work that took months (or years) can now be done in hours.

What makes these systems even more powerful is that they can incorporate sophisticated intelligence (and increasingly generative AI) to render the processes even more streamlined. Instead of predefining 10/100/1,000 rigid workflows, we can simply define the starting point, the end point, and the constraints. Then the system will respond to the user intelligently and dynamically. In the process, the user gets a fully personalized experience without supply chain managers having to manage and program vast complexity into their supply chain systems.

(continued on next page)

The end of process mapping (continued)

A good example of this is the Netflix interface. Every user sees a unique, personalized list of content based on their preferences, previous activity, and input. It would be silly for Netflix to offer a static set of predefined content to every user—yet this is what legacy supply chain systems do. Even worse, I have a client that spent millions (yes *millions*) of dollars to define every supply chain process from level one through level five. The systems integrator was more than happy to charge the client to do all this definition. Sadly, all this effort was wasted because it's not necessary in the age of generative AI-based process orchestration systems.

Are your digital transformations just ERP investments in disguise?

I've had more than one client tell me their digital transformation was consolidating many ERP systems down to a single instance. Reducing system complexity is good but let's not confuse that with transforming into a digital organization. Perhaps the most glaring reason digital transformations fail is that they over-index on the big-bang technology investment (for example, new system implementation, existing consolidation/rationalization, cloud migration). Similarly, most companies are good at the lift and shift of on-premise digital operations to Amazon Web Services/Microsoft Azure/Google Cloud Platform. But moving infrastructure to the cloud is only the first foundational step toward becoming a digital organization. The real work and opportunity of cloud migration is to evolve the legacy systems, in this case big ERP, so that you can take advantage of the powerful cloud infrastructure capabilities. At the time of writing (August 2023), AWS touts more than 200 different services. A truly digital organization would break up the lifted and shifted ERP systems into smaller components that use the myriad platform services these providers offer. However, just because you move your infrastructure to the cloud doesn't mean the business will suddenly start using the systems or that legacy ERP systems are even using the extensive cloud services.

Most digital transformations fail to consider the business adequately, and too much focus on an idealized state can guarantee failure. This just gives people the opportunity to poke holes in everything. As expected, IT is also one of the biggest impediments because, by definition, digital transformation will disrupt what they have done historically. In many cases, they won't do anything unless challenged, which is why there is a shift underway from chief information officer to chief digital officer. IT, and by extension the CIO, will grind you down until you lose credibility and/or waste millions of dollars. This dynamic can be clearly seen in digital supply chain designs where IT overextends its influence to the detriment of the business.

Not so ironically, as I was writing this chapter, I took a break to go to the local vegan coffee shop in my electric car.[35] Just as I was driving home, I received a call from a client who figured out that the ERP platform provider could not offer a pleasurable user experience for its sourcing managers. By chance, they found a provider who solves this problem and tried to bring them in. The IT group challenged them as if on cue by pointing to the ERP provider who claimed they could do it. First off, why is IT inserting itself into discussions about topics they know little about? How do they know what sourcing managers need? Have they ever done the job in question? Second, of course the ERP platform salespeople will say they can do whatever is asked of them; they are financially inclined to say yes to everything. My client said he was simply going to let the ERP-based solution get deployed, fail, and then in a year introduce the desired solution—all because he was tired of fighting IT. This highlights just how inept and wasteful IT can be when it comes to digitizing supply chains. Unless IT people have had specific training in supply chain design and operations, they have no business making decisions because they're either relying on the ERP software provider or talking with no knowledge. And supply chain leaders who accept this are putting a noose around their necks. The moment a disruption happens, that noose will tighten.

IT: have they earned a seat at the table?

Nearly every client I talk to tells me they are a [big ERP brand] shop. Their goal is to consolidate and streamline into a single provider—a singular place to go

---

[35] This detail may seem trivial but stick with me as it will be important later.

when something goes wrong. It's hard to argue with that logic. Of course, that logic only holds if the provider can fix the issue or add the feature in a timely way. This is where IT and big ERP stifle efficiency and introduce significant operational risk. If you're trying to become resilient to keep up with volatile supply and demand shocks or you're trying to lock up strategic partnerships (for exclusive tech or limited supply), you need timely insights. To get timely insights, you need real-time data and advanced analytical modeling (see Chapter III: *Intelligence: data underpins everything*). Clients tell me time and again how IT cannot give them these capabilities. The thinly veiled excuse is that big ERP has all the transactions, hence the data you need—just tell them what you require and it can be put into a report. That backward logic would be funny if it wasn't so risky to the business. In an era where our lives are influenced so heavily by algorithms (see Chapter VI: *Hacking AI and building algorithmic literacy*), the idea of building a report is silly. Do you want to make users manually search through thousands of data points in Excel or a dashboard to find outliers when simply pointing an analytical model at the data will do the same task in seconds? It's especially asinine given that there are many off-the-shelf solutions that do these tasks with ease.

A whole ecosystem of supply chain analytics tools has cropped up to provide specific insights that create the aforementioned value. IT has two typical and utterly lazy responses to this. First, they say (again), "We are a [big ERP] shop so they need to integrate with our environment." Of course, with API (application programming interface) infrastructure everywhere, this is becoming less of a legitimate excuse in the cloud era. Next, they will ask their big ERP account representative for ammunition to fend off the external provider. The telltale sign that they have done this is they will bring the [big ERP] software provider in to talk to the business and explain how it can or will be done in their existing system.[36] Of course this is a stall tactic, and when they come in, they will hear you out and then say that they have that coming in a future release. This wastes valuable time and money and frustrates everyone else involved.

---

[36] Of equal concern is that many IT teams have actually outsourced their operations, knowledge, and expertise to systems integrators/business process consultants. This creates a situation where there is little strategic thought and accountability retained within the organization. So "advice" for major technology decisions is being provided by those who stand to benefit and/or have mutually beneficial arrangements with the technology providers.

If the IT group wants to be a part of supply chain system design and operation, they need to earn their seat at the table. The default assumption is that because they are IT they have ownership of everything that is technology. But in the cloud era should that be the default position? When the collection of and use of supply chain data creates opportunity and competitive advantage, having an authoritarian entity—one with no knowledge of the nuances of the supply chain operations at hand—serving as the decider seems anachronistic if not derelict. Far too often, the IT group is allowed to veto a business decision. This is backward. When IT pushes the wrong technology into a solution, the business leaders, especially supply chain, should be able to veto the IT decision.

That is not to say IT groups don't have a role in a modern organization (though many question that). But they must prove they know about the supply chain without asking their big ERP sales rep for ammunition to use against the business. They should know the difference between reporting on a transaction and generating business insight. They should know the difference between OTIF (on time in full) and ATP (available to promise). They should know how and why managing supplier golden records is different than other golden records. And they should know the difference between supply planning and demand planning and the various inputs. If they can't answer these questions, they have no business making decisions or running your supply chain systems.

The other major challenge: the CIO

The CIO role has declined steeply over the past couple of decades. Specifically, over the past 30 years, the IT department has gone through a massive rationalization as a result of technological innovation. In the late 1990s CIOs were C-suite royalty strutting around as if they owned the place. They held the keys, literally and figuratively, to all the systems and data processing as enterprises started to embrace digitalization. These systems were complex, expensive, and required significant intervention to operate. Companies housed their systems in corporate data centers, staffed by armies of well-paid systems and network administrators, developers, and security experts. Purchasing new capacity required serious capital planning and timelines, as physical servers had to be ordered, shipped, and delivered. Then they needed to be installed in the data centers, networked, and readied for use. The CIO's army of highly paid technical experts managed all these systems at a rough estimate of one human to 10 servers. The emergence of cloud computing in the early 2010s completely gutted this structure as all these servers moved to the cloud, making the ratio one human to 100 servers. More recently with the move to computer platforms and self-managing/diagnosing systems, the ratio of IT humans to servers is one to 35,000. This shift has left the CIO organization reeling.

The changes described above are certainly material. However, there's an even bigger change that's impacted the CIO and IT: the fact that digital capabilities can no longer effectively be isolated into a single central department. Instead, they are increasingly located in the business. Joe Peppard, writer for *The Wall Street Journal,* is more blunt: "Here's the sad fact: having an IT department is exactly what will prevent companies from being innovative, agile, customer-focused and digitally transformed." He goes on to dismantle the "partnership engagement model," by which the IT group is a partner to the business— an order taker to the business.[37] The business provides its requirements to IT and they go away and source/build the solution and deliver it to the business (procurement people, does this sound familiar?). The problem is that the IT objectives are independent from the business. Peppard points out another key flaw: IT expenditures are defined up front in annual budgeting processes, which require business cases, specifications gathering, and estimates. Assuming budgets are approved, project plans and execution takes place over months and years. This is why going with big ERP is so attractive to CIOs; it meets their need to justify their existence based on the old way of working. But in a world of disruptions, that way of working snaps like an elephant sitting on a tree branch. In the platform era, success with digital has no correlation to managing the IT stack, uptime, or even user satisfaction. Instead, success needs to be measured in how technology contributes to the ability of the enterprise to meet customer expectations while operating in an efficient and economically viable manner. The implication is twofold. Digital resources need to be embedded with the business where they have a direct contribution and vested interest in the success of the outcomes. Correspondingly, the business has to be vastly upskilled in its ability to understand and adopt all this technological innovation.

---

[37] Peppard, Joe. "Get Rid of the IT Department." *The Wall Street Journal,* October 24, 2021. https://www.wsj.com/articles/get-rid-of-the-it-department-11637605133 (Accessed May 11, 2023).

Let's take HR as an example. The IT business partner approach has historically been to put in "human resource" systems such as Oracle's PeopleSoft (a truly archaic piece of technology) or Workday (a less archaic and only slightly less painful) HR system. But if you look at it from a business point of view, enterprises need "human capital" systems. Human capital management (HCM) is a vastly different approach that requires more nimbleness as new techniques emerge. Correspondingly, HCM requires the need for a core backbone platform that can integrate with a wide variety of point solutions that cover everything from recruiting to offboarding and all points in between. A hallmark of HCM systems is the need for greater intelligence. HCM systems need to be able to answer such questions as why do 70 percent of new hires leave within two years (creating a negative ROI on recruiting costs)? How do we increase organic recruiting? What would motivate an employee to work for a 100-year-old company? These questions can't be answered by legacy HR systems. Those rigid systems were built in a different century and meant to collect and manage basic employee information in a very linear manner. Instead, underpinning HCM is the need for deep third-party data integration with potential candidates, recruiting systems, LinkedIn, job sites, HR systems, and even CRM systems. In short, HCM requires the platform approach.

As most modern chief human resource officers have learned, those monolithic HR systems neither support nor reflect the reality of the current ways of working. There's now a constant reliance on outside contractors, a crucial need for data collection from many external sources, a requirement to train employees outside learning management systems (LMS), and significantly more varied and complicated workflows. Big HR systems struggle with all this complexity, which is why there's a huge explosion in HR tech as start-ups and newer platform players start to hit the market. Moreover, HCM requires building bespoke intelligence that takes advantage of all this data. Chief HR officers, like chief supply chain officers, are holding out for a hero. A hero that will provide a platform for easy data exchange (internally and externally), access to sophisticated data science libraries, and a smart "customized for me" interface.[38]

---

[38] The intelligent "customized for me" interface is representative of the idea of an approach where you don't predefine the UX, but rather create an experience that responds and learns based on what you do. So everyone gets a unique experience without it having to be coded.

It's pretty obvious why I am making this comparison (and I could have made it for other corporate functions). It is time for supply chain leaders to adopt a platform approach. The other key takeaway is that the CIO is not at the center of the digital universe. To punctuate this trend, Chris Howard, chief of research at Gartner, commented that, "Of all the roles that we cover, the role of CIO is in the most flux now."[39] For many years, and even still today, CIOs acted as a gatekeeper, citing "integration and security issues." But in the era of cloud platforms, democratized data, intelligence, and automation, there's much less that CIOs can control, and in many cases they can't even keep up. Gartner cites the percentage of technologists hired directly by the business units is 41 percent. That is a staggering amount and means that almost 50 percent of the CIOs' historical workforce now sits directly in the business.[40]

It's also important to highlight that we are in an era where people in the business have vastly more technical skills than ever before. Data management used to be the purview of the CIO—something they failed to deliver. Undeniably, we shouldn't be asking technical IT to make decisions about data governance. The business needs to take data from its raw form and turn it into intelligence, without IT involvement. For supply chain leaders, the problem with all this is that CIOs still have a death grip on supply chain systems. Otherwise, we wouldn't be suffering under the crushing weight of big ERP. To be fair to CIOs, big ERP is the only supplier set still inviting them on vacations and to golf outings. One thing is clear: anybody in supply chain today needs to be vastly more digitally and business savvy than previous generations. The significant rise in third-party management means supply chains need vastly more simple and agile systems. Good enough is no longer good enough. Letting CIOs, influenced by big ERP, dictate the path forward puts the enterprise at risk and will ultimately lead to disaster.

[39] Loten, Angus. "CIO Role in Flux as Businesses Embrace Tech." *The Wall Street Journal,* February 15, 2022. https://www.wsj.com/articles/cio-role-in-flux-as-businesses-embrace-tech-11645705801 (Accessed May 11, 2023).
[40] Loten, Angus. "CIO Role in Flux as Businesses Embrace Tech." *The Wall Street Journal,* February 15, 2022. https://www.wsj.com/articles/cio-role-in-flux-as-businesses-embrace-tech-11645705801 (Accessed May 11, 2023).

Architecting new supply chain tools

My fundamental argument for this book and the supply chain profession is that we need a new architecture built around third-party management to decrease risk and improve operational benefits (efficiency, agility, savings, and so on). To achieve this, we need a completely new infrastructure—one that centers the third party and data exchange. (See Figure 10: *A new supply chain architecture with third parties* on page 59.)

To attain this we need five interconnected rings of capability.[41] The first ring contains the data foundation, user experience, and integration. The data foundation will house golden records for third parties. It should also either contain or be linked to material and product golden records, and product design and engineering files. The user experience will be the single interface that gives the user the personalized view into our supply chain capabilities (the "ChatGPT" interface). This will be paired with process orchestration software that will allow us to define and manage workflows through our systems. The integration will take the form of an app store and/or middleware to manage the integration and communication between all the systems. The second layer is the cloud infrastructure. These are all the infrastructure-related libraries and technologies that enable us to connect, secure, and interact with the myriad third parties. By using cloud-native infrastructure we are unencumbered by the limitations of proprietary software. The third layer is related enrichments (for example, risk, ESG) coming from third-party solutions that we need to apply to all our data. Think of this as a filter that enriches all third-party data as it passes through. The final outer ring contains all the functional capabilities of the traditional plan, source, make, deliver, and reverse logistics capabilities. Here you may choose to use a traditional transactional system like an ERP for multiple areas of functionality or you may opt for newer and emerging start-ups for crucial capabilities such as planning. The key here is that data flows seamlessly from application to application in the outer ring, but it also flows seamlessly through the inner rings to make various connections to third parties.

---

[41] I chose the ring because all of these should seamlessly flow together and this seemed like the most logical.

Figure 10

A new supply chain architecture with third parties

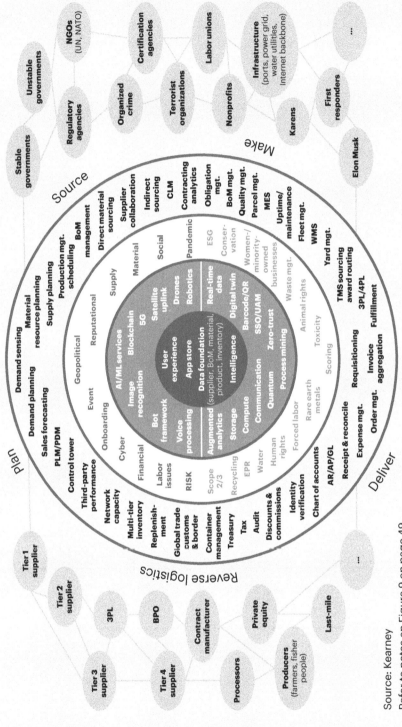

Source: Kearney

Refer to notes on Figure 9 on page 49.

Most importantly, in figure 10 you can see all the various third parties that need to interact or transact with the enterprise. I cannot stress this capability enough because if you look at the next figure you'll see that every third party has its own version of this circle diagram. (See Figure 11: *Multi-enterprise connectivity* on page 61.)

This visualization is exactly where the complexity of transacting and data exchange with third parties really becomes apparent. If we go back to the vaccine example I posed at the beginning you can start to see why it's so difficult. Every individual entity (vaccine manufacturer, air/sea/rail provider, trucking company, warehouse, injection site, healthcare provider, insurance company, government, and possibly NGOs) needs to exchange data with one another. And they all use disparate systems, none of which natively talk to one another, while some systems do not integrate at all. By incentivizing and rewarding third parties to share their data (and facilitating it seamlessly), we can close gaps of incomplete data, which in turn helps make us more secure.

The donut hole

The cloud revolution has changed the question of make versus buy. Now it's about make and buy. We've moved from the debate between single tool and best of breed to a platform *with* best of breed. This can best be described as a donut with frosting and sprinkles—the donut itself representing the platform and the icing and sprinkles representing the best of breed applications. That analogy works well because it shows that there is still a gap in the middle of the donut.

I frequently get pigeonholed as advocating best of breed over traditional suite solutions. My response is always the same: I am for a platform–ecosystem approach that incorporates the best of both. However, even the platform approach is not fully sufficient as it does not account for the unique use cases of every industry and company. I call this the hole in the donut. The only way to fill this in is to develop internally or co-develop custom, proprietary intelligence assets. In other words, to truly build the next-generation supply chain platform, every company will need to assemble some measure of bespoke intelligence assets to fill the donut hole. This is not something an off-the-shelf provider can deliver because it will never meet their incentive structure. Every platform and best-of-breed solution will only make money

...le; the key to scaling is uniformity. This is not a criticism—it is
...his rightly puts the burden on filling the donut hole on the company
...this is exactly why having strong digital capabilities is necessary.

...nd trace as a donut hole example

...trace (T&T) is an excellent articulation of the donut hole problem.
...&T capability is the ultimate revenue risk management because
... the brand. T&T does this by stitching together quality, compliance,
..., and customer experience through the use of data. The lowest
...is to ensure quality standards are met for every product. However,
... regulated products, quality must include requisite safety and
...eit prevention. That means quality needs to be tracked, tested, and
...from the source material through the production to the delivery.

...very global enterprise has various local, national, and global
...ry compliance responsibilities. These requirements manifest
...ves in the supply chain where every step needs to be validated
...e that all activities in the execution (sourcing, manufacturing, and
...ion) meet internal corporate and legal compliance. Once again,
...ogy and data capture with third parties is key throughout the process.

...ely, the customer wants the product or service when it is promised.
...ecret that the advent of same-day, two-hour delivery and the like have
...absurd expectations. Achieving this (assuming that remains the goal)
...s significant end-to-end information transparency at each step of the
...tion and distribution process. This enables significantly more robust
...ely information sharing to the end customer. Going back to the vaccine
...e, I wanted to pull the T&T data for the vaccine I put into my body. That
...be readily available by scanning the QR code on a vaccine card or
...directly connected to my electronic medical record sitting in the digital
...on my iPhone. Having T&T information plumbed into customer-facing
...systems allows us to give customers greater visibility into the supply
...that produced and delivered that product. The reverse is also true, but
...everse the data flow from the customer we can use it to forecast future
...nd, engage in preventative maintenance, and eventually reverse logistics
...e reuse or reincorporation of that product at its end of life.

Figure 11

Multi-enterprise connectivity

Vaccine supply chain example

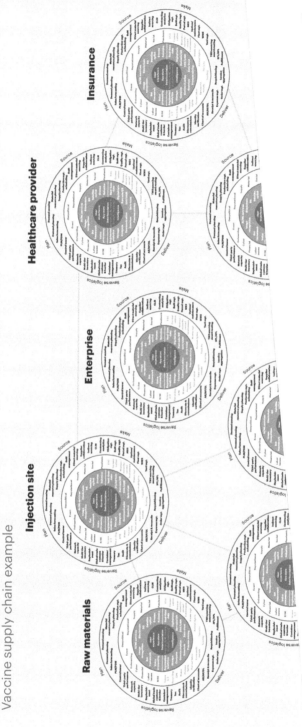

if it can so
a reality. T
itself. And

Track a

Track and
A robust
it protect
efficiency
threshold
for highl
counterf
validated

Nearly e
regulato
themse
to ensu
distribu
technol

Ultimat
It's no s
created
require
produ
and tir
examp
shoul
ideally
wallet
order
chain
if we
dema
for th

Trying to hit all these objectives (not even accounting for disruptions or just day-to-day friction) requires continuous improvement of the underlying platform services. In other words, there will never be an off-the-shelf type of solution. As with any operational data, T&T data can inform continuous cost and efficiency improvements and complexity reductions. I know what you're thinking—we do this in lean manufacturing already. That is good, and this is not meant to replace that, but rather to point out that when you have many third parties involved in manufacturing, packaging, and distribution, the T&T data collection and interpretation becomes an exponential problem.

Going back to the vaccine example, we can start to connect all these dots. As a customer I wanted to know if all the entities that handled the vaccine met quality, safety, and regulatory compliance standards. As a customer, none of this T&T was available to me. If there was a recall, how would that information have made it from the manufacturer to me? Moreover, had I experienced side effects how could I let Moderna, the medical profession, or regulators know? The data provides me with that chain of custody.

When Tony Soprano eats the donut (the limitation of digital T&T)

T&T technology has simultaneously both evolved and not evolved much over the past few decades. For many decades, we have used uniform device identification (UDI), global data synchronization network (GDSN), and barcodes to keep tabs on our SC operations. In the early 2000s innovations such as radio frequency identification (RFID), real-time locating systems (RTLS), and beacons (Bluetooth transmitters that send signals to nearby devices) hit the market, providing basic tracking, real-time identification, and location-based trigger alerts.[42] Increasingly we are moving to more smart device sensors communicating to the cloud (IoT, DLT, AI, NFC, NFI, drones). Automated signal processing and intelligence creation hold the promise of auto-capturing, processing, analyzing, and syndicating the requisite information to any system of consumption. This can include triggering smart

---

[42] Williams-McGhee, Lacey. "Beacon Technology and RFID Tags: Similarities and Differences." 7t Blog, January 13, 2020. https://7t.co/blog/beacon-technology-and-rfid-tags-similarities-and-differences/ (Accessed May 11, 2023).

contracts or completing transaction records such as change control, chain of custody, or signed-off validation.

However, there is a lot of hype about using this digital ledger technology (DLT), also known as blockchain, for T&T. Conceptually, blockchain as an immutable digital ledger to track every step of the T&T process is great. But it is important to understand that DLT is completely virtual so you need to connect it to a physical Internet-connected (IoT) device. And these devices need to embed into a container, pallet, or other such fixed place with the source material. However, most raw materials such as liquids, agricultural products, textiles, and other inanimate objects do not lend themselves to having physical devices connected to them, so we can put devices onto the holding/packaging containers.

This leads to the Tony Soprano problem. Tony Soprano, the fictional mafia boss from the HBO television show *The Sopranos,* was very adept at running fraudulent activities. Imagine this hypothetical scenario: a sustainable fishing company catches a premium batch of fish. They load it in a smart container and update the digital ledger. A local truck driver, under Tony's control, drives the fish to a warehouse where it is transferred and replaced with fish that looks the same, but is spoiled. The spoiled fish is processed in a plant, put into cans, and distributed to a store, with the ledger updated at each step along the way. Eventually, a customer buys the fish, eats it, and gets sick. The good news is we can quickly trace the evolution of the fish all the way to where it was caught, which makes the recall quicker and more targeted. Unfortunately, it doesn't account for the fact that the spoiled fish did not come from the fishing company in question. Meanwhile, Tony's guys take the sustainably caught fish and sell it for a premium. This is a textbook supply chain attack, an analog version of the SolarWinds attack.

Theoretically, we could solve part of the fish verification problem by taking pictures. However, that poses two crucial issues; the first is scale. There are an estimated 148 million tons of fish consumed each year.[43] Second, and

---

[43] "How much fish do we consume? First global seafood consumption footprint published," CORDIS Blog. September 28, 2018. https://phys.org/news/2018-09-fish-consume-global-seafood-consumption.html (Accessed May 11, 2023).

more concerning, is the production gap. With the fish example, we lose provenance in the gap between the product (fish) and the DLT because it requires a digital device not directly connected to the product to capture the relevant information. It is in that gap that Tony's guy can make his move. One could imagine a scenario where a picture of the fish is taken and the packing material is sealed with an IoT sensor that identifies if there is any tampering, temperature fluctuations, or deviations from the trucking route. But, that seems ridiculously complicated and expensive.

This example demonstrates that no matter how much technology we deploy, we must always account for the human factor. If we are to use DLT, or any technology, we must employ it in a way that accentuates its strengths. DLT excels when it is paired with IoT and machine intelligence. Instead of food, imagine a medical device product with IoT sensors in its major component systems. As soon as the device is assembled, every IoT sensor could start to write to the digital ledger. Then that activity is verified via some human and some machine intelligence. In this case, it would be more difficult for Tony's guys to swap out the component parts, which reduces the counterfeiting risk. If we revisit my opening story about the vaccine supply chain, what malfeasance could Tony Soprano have inflicted?

This is why we need to take a hacking approach to secure our supply chains. We must think critically about the physical-to-cyber transition (turning raw materials into manufactured products) or the reverse cyber-to-physical (embedding digital solutions into physical products). It is in these choke points that lives are at risk. This is also why we cannot rely solely on digital technologies to secure our supply chains. DLT will be part of the bigger solution, but we can't rely on it to be the sole solution—we still need humans in the mix. Specifically, we need human creativity to protect our supply chains because we are matching wits against human creativity (at least until the robot apocalypse).

Yesterday's legacy third-party data exchange: electronic data interchange (EDI)

"Even though it's [big ERP system] suboptimal, I chose it because I can sell it internally."

– VP of supply chain for CPG company

Created in the 1970s, the de facto standard for data exchange between companies and their suppliers—not even third parties—is electronic data interchange (EDI). For decades, organizations have relied on EDI to digitize paper invoices and to conduct purchase transactions. The obvious benefits are the processing efficiency and the elimination of human labor.[44] Unfortunately, in practice EDI is expensive, difficult for suppliers to adopt, and isn't terribly fault tolerant. By design, it's meant to be a hard coding of two organizations' systems. As a result, changes to those underlying systems will break the EDI link. Beyond that, EDI lacks the extensibility required for exchanging information in today's complicated supply chain landscape.

Today (and tomorrow), we need supply chain systems that facilitate collaboration across multi-enterprise data systems. We need to be able to constantly transfer changing information about invoices, POs, and the like (for example, expedite/push out/update/cancel). Plus, we need to extend data models in a dynamic way. Going back to the vaccine example, during the pandemic we suddenly needed to track the environmental controls of vaccines in transit. That is not a use case that EDI readily supports. In a crisis, we need to be able to quickly extend the data models in a way that does not require IT intervention or incur additional transaction fees. Despite the best intentions of EDI designers, what happens is that only top-tier suppliers get onboarded through EDI. The management of EDI orders reverts to spreadsheets and emails, which is self-defeating. Perhaps the biggest challenge to EDI is the cost; typically, there is tolling on the transaction, which defeats the purpose of data exchange. Charging money on data exchange is as old school as having a CIO. This is the difference between transferring a minimum amount of data for a transaction and truly collaborating with third parties.

---

[44] IBM. "EDI (Electronic Data Interchange)." IBM. https://www.ibm.com/topics/edi-electronic-data-interchange (Accessed May 11, 2023).

The need for an ever-growing data exchange is the future of supply chain operations, and a key part of this data collaborative future is deeper integration into core operational systems, whether on the manufacturing floor, warehouse, truck, or customer location. More specifically, we need to build a data exchange platform that's designed for bidirectional data collaboration. Historically, the supply chain is done once the products get to the customer (save for defects and returns). However, the rise of smart products means that they need to constantly "phone home." This requires our supply chain infrastructure to consume this reverse data, whether sending updates to the customer product or simply processing information from said device. For example, consider the consumables that come in smart packaging. When the weight of the package hits a certain threshold, a signal could be sent back to auto-order more of the product or at least notify the planning systems to proactively preposition inventory.

Enabling bidirectional supply chain data exchange with third parties is a use case beyond what any ERP could handle. ERPs have many decades of legacy data models to contend with, but the data models will be ever changing in the bidirectional supply chain. Therefore, we need to start making third-party connections at the cloud layer instead of the ERP. We also have to understand data exchange from the third-party point of view.

Hacking tools: five takeaways

— The ERP is dead; stop waiting for it to evolve.

— Embrace the cloud infrastructure as your new supply chain backbone.

— Design with third-party data exchange at the core.

— Demand that IT and the CIO earn their participation.

— Make sure your digital transformation is not an ERP upgrade in disguise.

— Bonus: keep Tony Soprano out of your supply chain.

Chapter V
People: preparing practitioners for the digital zeitgeist

"Amateurs hack systems, professionals hack people."

– Bruce Schneier, renowned computer security expert and author

"My client took agile and corporatized it."

– Anna Kraft, Kearney partner

As evidenced from the President Reagan assassination attempt, the Secret Service agents used their bodies as shields to protect the president. Obviously, that was not the best use of human assets. Bulletproof vests, better crowd control, and movement flows could have prevented the shooter from ever getting near the president. Today's supply chains have the same problem, as evidenced by the immense human capital invested to react to every disruption. Instead of deploying human assets where they are most effective, we have them doing the work that intelligence and tools could be doing far better—tasks like fraud detection, data transfer (cutting and pasting or manually importing or exporting data), T&T, reporting, filling out or responding to RFPs, and so on. However, to redeploy our human assets we need to better train them and create a culture that rewards useful work.

The training fallacy: error proofing versus upskilling

"Even turkeys fly in a hurricane."

— Peter Weis, CIO and supply chain executive

Every year I am forced to take a cybersecurity awareness training. Technically, I have to do it twice—once for Kearney and once for Norwich University, where I teach graduate history classes and direct capstone projects. These training courses are self-paced and delivered online through a learning management system. I look forward to this activity; I am curious to see how quickly I can get through the module without reading or watching any of the content. When one of the videos starts, I try to bypass it by moving the cursor all the way to the end with my finger or mouse. My record for completing the "training" is three minutes and twenty-seven seconds. If I can click through a training with minimal effort, that begs a fundamental question: why are we doing this pointless exercise? I know I am not alone because I ask everyone the same question and I have yet to find someone who doesn't do some version of this. And if these trainings were so good then ransomware wouldn't be such a significant issue. Despite the preponderance of cybersecurity training, ransomware attacks run rampant. It's reported that 76 percent of companies have been the victim of ransomware attacks in the past two years alone and most of them have actually paid the ransom.[45]

In a shining example of how bad cybersecurity awareness is, Singapore's government technology agency undertook a test to see if they could get their colleagues to click on phishing emails. Some were written by hand and others by a machine-generated algorithm. Shockingly, more people ("by a significant margin") clicked on the machine-generated emails. This was by no means a definitive study, but it is an indicator of the efficacy of these tools when employed for negative purposes.[46]

If you choose to offer corporate cybersecurity training, proceed at your own risk. Here are some highlights (or lowlights) of what one can learn from common cybersecurity modules:[47]

— "Phishing tricks users into providing sensitive information to cybercriminals via email, text, WhatsApp, and other media."

---

[45] Rubin, Andrew. "A practical approach to building resilience with zero trust." VentureBeat, August 13, 2022. https://venturebeat.com/security/a-practical-approach-to-building-resilience-with-zero-trust/ (Accessed May 11, 2023).
[46] Newman, Lily Hay. "AI is Sending People Creepy Emails From Their Own Accounts." Wired, August 7, 2021. https://www.wired.com/story/ai-phishing-emails/ (Accessed May 11, 2023).
[47] Now if you find these tips useful, then that's good, I've helped you practice for this year's "cybersecurity awareness training."

— "Hackers use various techniques to trick you."

— "Phishing is associated with virus infections, ransomware, identity theft, and data theft."

— "Attackers may also use your computer to attack others."

Here's what users are supposed to do:

— "Take a close look. Examine carefully. Be suspicious."

— "Falling victim to phishing can be avoided if you give emails and requests for information a close examination. It pays to be extra cautious."

— "Each part of an email is a decision point."

— "Look for red flags relating to the sender of the email."

These anecdotes are merely descriptors of what to look for and what to do if you find it. They are patently obvious to anybody who consumes news, social media, or warnings from big tech providers. Nothing in these statements is wrong. In fact, they are technically correct. Unfortunately, they do nothing to make us any safer than before we took the module.

These course excerpts represent a key differentiator between "learning digital" and "doing digital." Specifically, these trainings are geared to the least common denominator of risk, email, and collaboration platforms (for example, WhatsApp) to maximize audience applicability. The glaring problem is twofold. First, what about all the other threat vectors that are not email or collaboration tools, such as social engineering or fake websites? Second, each of us uses a wide variety of messaging platforms in a typical day and the threats within each are unique. For example, I will log into four different email accounts (personal, work, education, legacy email), five collaboration platforms (Teams, Slack, Facebook Messenger, WhatsApp, LinkedIn messenger), and countless app-specific messaging platforms (banking, YouTube, Yelp) in the course of a day. And that's just me. There are numerous other platforms—Twitter, TikTok, Pinterest, WeChat, and so on—so how can 15 minutes adequately prepare me against all the possible threats coming from each of these applications?

More importantly, with the rise of sophisticated innovations such as natural language generation (NLG), machine learning, and large language models like Chat GPT, many of the "learnings" and "recommended actions" in the trainings don't hold up. A recent study found that "advances in natural language generation have resulted in machine-generated text that is increasingly difficult to distinguish from human-authored text." The authors say that the application of these technologies is getting so sophisticated that each message can be auto-customized for each target and can spear phish at scale.[48] If that doesn't scare you, consider that ChatGPT is already being used to create spam and ransomware.[49] That means that all the cybertraining that teaches us to look for red flags is useless because the red flags no longer exist.

Setting aside cybersecurity, there are broader educational concepts at play when we look at corporate training. Research into memory retention shows that when presented with new material, we instantaneously lose 70 percent of it. Without a structural intervention, the remaining 30 percent mostly slips away over the next month.[50] So the goal with training is to slow the process of forgetting.[51] Imagine all the in-person training days, lectures, webinars, podcasts, and learning modules we've taken. Think about how much of that information has evaporated from our collective consciousness. Educational researchers point out the fallacy of corporate training: "Science proves that our brains can't retain information and knowledge by watching videos, reading manuals, or listening to hours of training sessions over Zoom."[52] Why then are we engaging in corporate learning programs that are built on the idea that exposure to material and pretend engagement (rote quizzes) teaches us something that we will retain?[53] The annual cybertrainings I take each year suffer from these delusions of learning.

[48] Crothers, Evan, Japowicz, and Viktor, Herna. "Machine Generated Text: A Comprehensive Survey of Threat Models and Detection Methods." ArXiv preprint arXiv:2210.07321, 2022. https://arxiv.org/pdf/2210.07321.pdf (Accessed May 11, 2023).

[49] Goodin, Dan. "ChatGPT is enabling script kiddies to write functional malware." Ars Technica, January 6, 2023. https://arstechnica.com/information-technology/2023/01/chatgpt-is-enabling-script-kiddies-to-write-functional-malware/ (Accessed May 11, 2023).

[50] Brown, Peter C., et al. *Make It Stick: The Science of Successful Learning*, 18 (London, England: Belknap Press, 2014).

[51] Brown et al. *Make It Stick*, 28.

[52] Caucci, Sam. "How Learning Really Works: A Conversation with Peter C. Brown." 1Huddle Blog, October 27, 2020. https://blog.1huddle.co/how-learning-really-works-a-conversation-with-peter-c.-brown (Accessed May 11, 2023).

[53] Brown et al. *Make It Stick*, 10-11.

The most egregious problem with corporate training is the pursuit of "errorless learning." Companies need to attest to customers, clients, board members, regulators, and even the public that they are compliant with whatever competency (cybersecurity, ethics, ESG, and the like). If a company can't show mastery of a particular topic like cybersecurity, then how can it attest to being secure? So all the material and testing is constructed to create no errors to "prove" sufficient mastery of the topic. Unfortunately, this ensures that no meaningful learning occurs because enterprising users can simply bypass the training with minimal effort.[54]

Replacing "training" with actual learning

To move beyond corporate busy work (training), we need to apply five pedagogical concepts that move us toward teaching people. Learning must be social, failure driven, provide time for reflection, generative, and have personal meaning to the employees. In the context of digital, we need to apply these five concepts in a practical hands-on manner, often referred to as "experiential learning."

1. Training must be social

To effectively train people on digital we need to enable it as a social and cultural activity. Educational researchers have established a definitive link between learning and social activity. They explain that the brain is an implicitly social organ that technically learns from interactions and environmental stimuli. In fact, the brain craves interpersonal stimuli as a learning channel. This is why in-person meetings and trainings can feel so much more useful because the brain is being constantly activated and absorbing information that is not available on a conference call or Zoom meeting.[55] As an example, consider my friend Mike Cadieux, who went down (I mean *way* down) the blockchain/crypto/NFT rabbit hole. He learned the basics pretty quickly on his own. But sharing with me, and the following discussions and predictions of where this technology could go, spurred the learning for him. I knew even less

---

[54] Brown et al. *Make It Stick*, 90.
[55] Nasir, N. S., Lee, C. D., Pea, R., & McKinney de Royston, M. (2021). Rethinking Learning: What the Interdisciplinary Science Tells Us. Educational Researcher, 50(8), 557–565. https://doi.org/10.3102/0013189X211047251 (Accessed May 11, 2023).

than he did, but the social connection made me want to learn it with him. The amount of time we spent discussing this and the number of text messages were voluminous. But the shared learning experience and excitement took us further than we could have ever done individually. We're now experiencing the dynamic of social learning with the explosion of generative AI. ChatGPT and its antecedents have been around for a few years and the public took very little notice. But once it entered popular culture it seems as though we can't go five minutes without someone referencing it or creating LinkedIn posts wondering if it will replace all our jobs. This creates a reinforcing dynamic where more people go to check out the tool.

If we think about the act of hacking, it's deconstructing a tool or system to its component parts to learn the individual pieces and then putting it back together in a new way. This is exactly how the human brain works during the learning process.[56] We need to create time that encourages learners to explore what they find interesting, and to share that with others. Again, this is what hackers do; they seek to find vulnerabilities for things that could or should be different, then they share their findings.

2. Training must be failure driven

It's all fun and games until you show up at work as a cat.

Watching Texas lawyer Rod Ponton attend a civil forfeiture case hearing over Zoom with a cat filter on is one of the most iconic, if not hilarious, moments of the pandemic. In February 2021, late night comics pilloried Mr. Ponton for his inability to understand how to use the technology, knowing neither how the cat filter got turned on or, more importantly, how to turn it off. It's impossible to watch that clip without laughing, despite the perfunctory nature of the hearing. At one point, Mr. Ponton assures the court that he is in fact "… here live. I'm not a cat." After about a minute, Ponton removed the filter and returned to business. Herein lies the power of digital technology and the pitfall of not having the requisite literacies. But it's also a useful educative moment for Mr. Ponton, who presumably learned how to turn off the cat filter when

[56] Immordino-Yang, M. H. (2016). Emotion, Sociality, and the Brain's Default Mode Network: Insights for Educational Practice and Policy. Policy Insights from the Behavioral and Brain Sciences, 3(2), 211. https://doi.org/10.1177/2372732216656869 (Accessed May 11, 2023).

starting a Zoom call or at least to check if it's on before launching Zoom. So his "failure" created a learning moment he (and hopefully we) will never forget. (See Figure 12: *I am not a cat* on page 76.)

One of the flashiest pieces of Silicon Valley jargon to make its way into the corporate lexicon is "failing fast." It refers to a start-up tech company's ability to develop something, test it out, and abandon it quickly if it doesn't work. In Silicon Valley, failing fast is a badge of honor and something to be celebrated. In fact, Alphabet takes pride in the fact that most of its products are failures (Circles, Wave, Orkut, Hangout, Answers, Dodgeball, Notebook, and many more). Eliminating the fear of failure paves the way to learn and increase digital competency.

The Super Mario effect
YouTube science sensation and former NASA engineer Mark Rober did a 2015 TEDx Penn talk entitled *The Super Mario Effect: Tricking Your Brain into Learning More*. Rober invited his followers to play a simple game he created that claimed to teach anyone to program. He didn't tell the 50,000 people who played that this was an experiment. When users completed the game, they were randomly shown one of two messages. One read simply, "Please try again." The other was, "That didn't work. You lost five points. You now have 195 points. Please try again." The points were fake, contained no value, and were not shared with anyone else. However, the difference in the messaging produced two dramatically different outcomes. Sixty-eight percent of people who saw the no-penalty message completed the challenge. However, only 52 percent of the people who lost five points per failure finished the challenge. He points out that the non-penalized users tried the puzzle two-and-a-half times more, thus increasing the learning process.

Rober uses the above findings as an opportunity to reframe the learning process as a video game, specifically *Super Mario Brothers*. He argues that when playing a video game, failures are part of the learning process and users accept them as part of the experience. The failures lead to one learning after another: jump here, duck there, run faster, and so on. He points out that when life in the real world goes awry, "failure and doubt start to creep in." Instead, he extols people to keep their focus on the endgame, in this case saving the princess. And, for each of life's challenges to treat them "like video

Figure 12
"I am not a cat"

Source: "Kitten Zoom Filter Mishap," 394th District Court of Texas - Live Stream, https://www.youtube.com/watch?v=KxlPGPupdd8, accessed July 17, 2023

games." By doing this it shifts the focus to the game and not how dumb one might look.[57]

The authors of *Make it Stick: The Science of Successful Learning*—Peter C. Brown, Henry Roediger III, and Mark A. McDaniel—provide scientific evidence to support Rober's claims. They blame Western culture for creating an environment where learners internalize errors as a marker of failure and believe they must be avoided at all costs. This is a dynamic that is often reinforced by instructors.[58]

The aversion to failure is reinforced by instructors who wrongly believe that when "learners are allowed to make errors, it's the errors that they will learn."[59] They go on to point out that this poisons experimentation and risk-taking, which are crucial for the learning process. Even worse, this can seep into the subconscious to the point that you're spending more effort avoiding mistakes and failure instead of solving the problems to build learning capacity.[60] Taken together, in a corporate environment where "failing fast" is not part of the culture, this creates a reinforcing effect. People fear failing and set their objectives (especially learning objectives) to what they can achieve comfortably. Rober argues that failure should be a badge of honor and a driver to continue attacking the problem by using different solution techniques.[61] It's a journey of learning exploration instead of a rote answer or empty calorie learning.

If we agree that failing is how we learn digital skills, then the logical conclusion is that we should include failure as a KPI. We should be able to highlight what we attempted, what failed and why, and quantify it. This gets us down the path of activity versus productivity. Producing activity is a simply a series of safe actions designed to show that one has been actively engaged doing tasks, regardless of efficacy. But there is no guarantee that any of those actions net any value for the enterprise or the employee. This is marked by employees who want to complicate discussions, talk endlessly about a project, or postpone

---

[57] Rober, Mark. "The Super Mario Effect: Tricking Your Brain into Learning More." TED, Recorded June 2018. Video, https://www.ted.com/talks/mark_rober_the_super_mario_effect_tricking_your_brain_into_learning_more (Accessed May 11, 2023).
[58] Brown et al. *Make It Stick*, 90.
[59] Brown et al. *Make It Stick*, 90.
[60] Brown et al. *Make It Stick*, 91.
[61] Brown et al. *Make It Stick*, 7.

taking action (basically what middle managers do when they kill digital transformations). By comparison, if we look at productivity, that is a series of actions that add value. Oftentimes the value is created from failing. Consider, 99 percent of a hacker's work can be regarded as a "failure." But each step along the path is very productive because it's enumerating the defenses and finding vulnerabilities until they finally break through and land on a vulnerability to exploit.

3. Training must provide reflection time

A key part of learning is reflection: taking time to ask the questions of what went well, what could have gone better, and why. In military circles this is known as the debrief. B-2 stealth bomber pilot Bill Crawford did a TED Talk in which he recounted his time flying 36-hour, nonstop missions from Missouri (Whiteman Air Force Base in the US) all the way to Baghdad and back without landing. He recounts doing that mission, landing, and going straight into a debrief. He breaks down the mission as 39 percent time spent planning, 58 percent in mission execution, and 3 percent in debriefing. Despite the disparity, he asserts that the debrief is where the learning and improvement comes from. Their debriefs consisted of five questions:

— What happened?

— What went right?

— What went wrong?

— Why?

— What can we learn from this?

He describes the debrief as where the true learning takes place. Further, he explains that his squadron set up an egalitarian culture free from blame or judgment, where ego is left behind and the only thing that matters is learning from mistakes, practicing, and getting better.[62] US fighter pilot

[62] Crawford, Bill. "Kill and Survive: A Stealth Pilot's Secrets of Success." TEDx Rexburg, Recorded January 2, 2016. Video, TEDx Rexburg, https://tedxrexburg.com/bill-crawford-2/ (Accessed May 11, 2023).

Mark Fogel describes a similar debrief process in which his squadron spends hours reviewing performance data for 10 minutes of actual action.[63] What is sad and shocking is that corporate training lacks any time for reflection, opting for scale, repeatability, and error-free outcomes. If we are going to truly train people in risk management, we need to do deep-dive case studies into the major security breaches and take the time to process and internalize them.

4. Training must be generative

Entrepreneur and self-proclaimed evil doer Jeff Jonas ran an experiment with his girlfriend's son and cousins at a party. He bought five 300-piece jigsaw puzzles for the kids to solve. However, he made some alterations:

— Puzzle 1: he removed 30 pieces, leaving 270 out of 300

— Puzzle 2: he removed 100 pieces, leaving 200 out of 300

— Puzzle 3: he removed 150 pieces, leaving 150 out of 300

— Puzzle 4: he removed 294 pieces, leaving 6 out of 300

— Puzzle 5: was a copy of puzzle 1, where he removed 270 pieces, leaving 30 out of 300

He then mixed them all together and dropped them on the table, telling the kids nothing of his malfeasance. It took the kids 22 minutes before they figured out that there was a duplicate. At 35 minutes they realized that some pieces were missing. At 37 minutes they started to determine some of the imagery—people sitting on a porch playing banjo, a scene from puzzle #3, the one with half the pieces missing. At 2 hours and 10 minutes, the kids realized that there were four puzzles and at 2 hours and 18 minutes they figured out that it was four puzzles with a few random pieces thrown in.

This was a gigantic exercise in generation learning. Jonas didn't have to tell the kids what the problem was. They thought they were solving a jigsaw, but in the

[63] Fogel, Mark. "The Culture of a Fighter Squadron." TED, recorded November 2018. Video, https://www.ted.com/talks/mark_fogel_the_culture_of_a_fighter_squadron (Accessed May 11, 2023).

process he was helping them build context-generation skills of observation. Most learning management systems are the opposite of generative learning; they start by providing the answer and then quiz you on whether you read it.[64] In generative learning, the goal is to find that "aha moment," such as when the kids realized that the jigsaw challenge was much more than simply putting together a puzzle. Learning digital is all about finding that "aha moment," successfully making the API connection, getting the database to return what you were looking for, or simply having the information at your fingertips with the press of a button. This happens because we teach the brain to struggle with the technical challenge over time until we achieve that moment of clarity. Then the repetition randomly over time keeps it present.

Solving incomplete puzzles that require research, observation, pattern building, and social collaboration is what underpins highly popular alternate reality games (ARGs). According to Wired contributing editor Clive Wilson, "ARGs are designed to be clue-cracking, multiplatform scavenger hunts." ARGs are often used for promotional ploys such as movies, television shows, books, and other consumer products (including the launch of the Audi A3 car).[65] What makes ARGs relatively unique is that they are free to play and don't require special equipment like video games, so there are low barriers to entry. They are great for collaborative problem-solving in that a cryptic clue is "dropped," then you work together to scour the online world and all types of media to uncover more clues and solve the mystery or, as Wilson notes, find signals in the noise. Non-technical users will quickly learn new digital skills such as scraping and algorithmic text analysis to comb through the noise and make connections. Social collaboration and rewards are key to this as users build street cred among the community. All these dynamics are self-reinforcing in that one success leads to another, which motivates users to keep going.[66]

[64] Jonas, Jeff. "Context Computing." September 29, 2015. Video, O'Reilly. https://www.oreilly.com/content/context-computing/ (Accessed May 11, 2023).
[65] Kiley, David. "A New Kind of Car Chase." Bloomberg, May 15, 2005. https://www.bloomberg.com/news/articles/2005-05-15/a-new-kind-of-car-chase (Accessed May 11, 2023).
[66] It is important to note that the ARG paradigm can lead to seeing clues that don't actually exist and/or be co-opted by bad actors (e.g., trolls, political operatives, anti-government actors) to create quests that don't actually exist. A scary, real-world example of this is the Qanon phenomenon. Quoting Wilson again, "cyberspace facilitates the obsessive joint scrutiny of everything, from TV shows to knitting patterns to the belief that reptilians walk among us … if players solve one puzzle, they crave the fun of tackling more, more, and more. But they can wind up seeing puzzles that aren't puzzles." Wilson, Clive. "QAnon Is the Most Dangerous Game You've Never Played." Wired, May 15, 2005. https://www.wired.com/story/qanon-most-dangerous-multiplatform-game/ (Accessed May 11, 2023).

5. Training must be personal

We are not robots. It is important to understand that teaching humans is different than teaching machines (we'll talk about training them later). While that may sound obvious, consider how corporate training is communicated (dictated). Training programs are usually announced as a detached task—"You must complete this course by a certain date"—with requisite follow-up notifications until the task is completed. Or the training requirement is communicated as part of a digital transformation whereby employees are supposed to complete a predefined list of classes in a mandatory (or semi-mandatory) set of meticulously tracked learning objectives or pathways. Then training plans are laid out and progress measured as part of job performance. This is all fine, except that human learning is impacted by the human condition. If people are sick, stressed due to a deadline, just had a fight with their spouse, worried about their kids, or under other similar pressure, their ability to learn will be affected. These external variables will further influence the learning experience with the content.[67] In other words, learning is a key part of the human experience and is improved by cultural and social factors.

For learning to truly stick, each learner needs the content to be personalized to them. The learning objective must be for the individual to extract the key ideas and internalize them into a mental model that works for them.[68] To do this there must be a steady accumulation of knowledge and a relevance to one's life experience. This allows the learner to reflect on and mentally rehearse how it applies to a particular situation or debrief on the lessons learned.[69] Naturally this creates a scale problem when an enterprise needs to train anywhere from 50,000 to 200,000 employees—so the question is, how do we personalize training at scale?

Successful learning occurs when new material is presented in a personalized manner followed by frequent quizzes of that material offered up at random times. This forces the learner to reach back and apply previously learned information, interweaving two or more topics and randomness.[70] A key tenet

---

[67] Gail Boldt & Kevin M. Leander (2020) Affect Theory in Reading Research: Imagining the Radical Difference, Reading Psychology, 41:6, 515-532, DOI: 10.1080/02702711.2020.1783137.
[68] Brown et al. *Make It Stick*, 6.
[69] Brown et al. *Make It Stick*, 18, 27.
[70] Brown et al. *Make It Stick*, 51.

of learning is knowing what you will be doing with knowledge later. If you know you want to break into someone's website or physical building, you're going to undertake a series of learnings based on that singular objective.

Too many corporate learning objectives (and corporate objectives, for that matter) are designed for mass consumption and focused on the least common denominator ("This is what a suspicious email looks like."). If you know the objective is to get me to click on a link to install malware, you must start by learning anything and everything you can about me. Me clicking the email is the objective that the mental model builds on and the retrieval of all information will be in support of that.[71] (See sidebar: *Gamification is not the answer* on page 83.)

Teaching people to spear phish

Let's bring the social, failure-driven, reflective, generative, personalized learning concepts together to meet a learning objective: supply chain cybersecurity. I started this chapter by pointing out the futility of cybersecurity training as it is done today. I propose reversing the training paradigm by applying the learning methodologies above and digital competencies to this problem. Instead of reading about what makes a suspicious email, why do we not train people to write phishing emails? This is the modern equivalent of the saying, "If you give a person a fish, they eat for a day, but if you teach them to fish, they eat forever."[72] When you explain what suspicious emails look like, you're giving that person a fish. Instead, we need to teach people to phish, or more specifically, we need to teach them how to spear phish.

Spear phishing is a very targeted attack that attempts to trick a user into giving up their account credentials or allows for impersonating them. Successful spear phishing or cyber compromise anywhere in the supply chain puts every tier and node at risk because of the implied trust therein (as described in the SolarWinds attack). The targeted spear phishing attack uses information about the person to make the notification more personalized. A money-making offer from the Crown Prince of Nigeria is probably not legitimate. Similarly,

---

[71] Brown et al. *Make It Stick*, 57.
[72] In 1986 an article about bodywork in "Yoga Journal" (Number 66) ascribed the saying to Lao-Tzu: "If you give a hungry man a fish, you feed him for a day, but if you teach him how to fish, you feed him for a lifetime." https://quoteinvestigator.com/2015/08/28/fish/

Gamification is not the answer

Do an RFP for corporate training and inevitably the term gamification will come up in the responses. It's used as an umbrella term to imply that assigning rewards and points will create meaningful and sustained engagement. Gamification terms gained popularity in the corporate training realm after Dan Tapscott and Anthony D. Williams' book *Wikinomics: How Mass Collaboration Changes Everything*. *Wikinomics* pushed organizations to harness the power of the crowd, especially those outside the enterprise itself. It spurred companies to become good at collaboration. Gamification quickly became core to increasing and sustaining collaboration. Terms like leaderboards, ratings, badges, voting, and the like quickly emerged. Almost overnight every app, tool, and initiative became "gamified" to promote team collaboration, motivation, and engagement. Yet those promises remain unfulfilled.

Gamification has long been applied to the educational realm. Older folks like myself will remember analog reading contests during elementary school where everyone in the class was encouraged to compete to see who could read the most books. Younger folks may remember "accelerated learner" programs, which took this to the digital realm. In both versions the goal is to get kids to read more, which is laudable. So kids pick books based on their progress and quizzes. In return, readers are rewarded with public accolades (levels, progress indicators, and so on) and given recommendations for additional books. This is using gamification to get students to read more. The problem is that the whole model is based on increasing the consumption of books, so it pushes the student to do what the teacher, or administrator, or parent wants, but doesn't build a love of reading. As long as you can answer the quiz questions at the end you move along; we read to the quiz, not to foster a love of reading. Does this sound familiar? This is the problem with corporate training (say cybertraining), where we're working to pass the quiz to check the box and not learning anything about protecting the enterprise.

(continued on next page)

Gamification is not the answer (continued)

Imagine a young sixth grade student who didn't particularly enjoy reading or doing schoolwork. The teacher, let's call her Ms. Reynolds, put the student in one of these analog reading contests where students were required to do a write-up for each book they read. As it turns out, our student was out sick for a whole week just after the reading contest started. Alone at home and bored—this was pre-Internet—this student started thinking about how they could participate in the reading contest without taking the time to read the books. It occurred to them that all they needed to do was read the synopsis on the back, rewrite it in their own words, and submit that as evidence of having read the book. That student handed in 12 of these and won the contest having read none of the books and absorbed absolutely nothing from the exercise. This is the problem with gamification: we simply try to solve for what the gamemaster designed, instead of learning.

Gamification gives the supposed learner the illusion of choice. But they are simply choosing from a predetermined set of options created by the gamemaster; the learner doesn't learn, they simply operate within the constructs of the artificial game. And the more enterprising users will try to reverse-engineer or even hack the game to see if they can outwit both the game and the gamemaster, like our hypothetical sixth grader or me when I take my two annual cybersecurity "trainings."

Further, gamification assumes that everyone within the enterprise will compete for badges, recognition, and non-monetary rewards as a way of driving activity in a LMS or even adoption of a new tool. But this lacks a proper incentive structure. There is a difference between Starbucks offering me 20 bonus stars if I order three days in a row, where I will get the reward of a free drink, versus taking seemingly useless training courses simply to get a virtual badge next to my name on a site that nobody visits.

a notification that I won the lottery is equally suspicious. Why? I don't play the lottery, and I know that Nigeria is a federal republic consisting of 36 states, that dynastic titles vary by sub-region, and include Emir, Aku Uka, Ohnoyi, Ohimege, Oba, Onije, Ovie, and Obi, none of which is "Prince."[73]

Here's an example of how vulnerable humans are to spear phishing. Let's take Jane, a bookkeeper at Acme Electronics. Acme Electronics makes wiring harnesses that go into nearly every printed circuit board. They would be a tier 4 supplier to most high-tech companies or a tier 5 supplier for automotive companies. Jane is vegan, likes high-end fashion, and has a dog. If I want to disrupt a large automotive company, I simply trace their supply chain down to Acme Electronics, then I look on LinkedIn for who is their bookkeeper. Then I "friend" Jane. I find her on Facebook and see if I can get to her through a friend of a friend to learn as much about her as possible. If all else fails, I can purchase her core personal identifying information (assuming Google doesn't just feed it to me) such as address, phone number, and email. I can also purchase web browsing history from Jane's neighborhood through a data broker. Then I simply deanonymize the data to see where Jane has browsed and transacted on the Internet (yes, it's that easy). I write a phishing email offering a vegan dog food and get her to click on the link—when she does that I can compromise her computer. Once I've compromised her computer, I can compromise other Acme computers because Acme is trusted by the next supplier, ABC Systems. And I can continue with the next provider up the food chain until I get all the way up to the prized target. Even if I don't make it to the high-value target, compromising a tier 1 supplier and changing the banking information could easily net me a couple million dollars. This could have a catastrophic effect for the tier 1 supplier and the original equipment manufacturer (OEM) that might have to provide the money to fill the gap.

Let's test your knowledge. If you wanted to spear phish me, how would you approach it? I've left plenty of clues throughout the text and footnotes. In fact, feel free to attempt to spear phish me after you've read this book.

Building cybersecurity awareness and capabilities should be a pleasurable exercise because it's something that helps all of us in our personal lives as

---

[73] "Nigerian traditional rulers." Wikipedia. https://en.wikipedia.org/wiki/Nigerian_traditional_rulers (Accessed May 11, 2023).

much as our work lives. So theoretically this is win–win, yet we screw it up by dumbing down the content. Cybersecurity is getting worse, and learning how to protect ourselves should be something useful instead of a corporate mandate. Digital competencies are exactly the same.

How do we help people build digital competencies?

The short answer is we don't have the learning tools we need. Consider that digital is learned through the act of doing. And doing means talking to others, sharing ideas, exploring the art of the digital possible, testing software, attending conferences, and just about any other activity that is in the realm of exploration, experimentation, and embracing these topics. Escape rooms are a great way to teach people crucial problem-solving skills, and they meet the pedagogical elements identified above (social, failing, filling in gaps, and reflection). Eventually, I predict we will have digital escape rooms that challenge people to employ and reinforce learning of key digital concepts. ARGs, as described above, have all the hallmarks for learning and applying digital skills. They still need to be adapted and applied to the corporate environment. Most importantly, they need to be personalized to an audience of one.

People reach out to me all the time asking for a recommendation for the best kind of tool for this or that. I always sidestep the question, using a highly specialized consulting evasion technique. Instead, I give them a list of all the providers I know and encourage them to talk to them and do the evaluation. I do this because I'm not in the business of crowning winners and losers; that is a fool's errand and something that should be stopped (but won't because there is money to be made). What works for one healthcare company won't work for another. I want every organization to build the muscle to do the evaluations themselves—that is how we grow digital competency. If we're simply relying on the analysts and consultants, then we're offloading a key literacy development to people who aren't invested in the outcome. The question that follows is how do I hear about all these tools or where do I go to find out about them? That is a question I love and answer vociferously. My recommendation is to talk to a vast swath of people. Talk to competitors, non-competitors, founders, venture capitalists, influencers, or anybody who writes about these topics. Attend conferences, build new connections, talk to speakers and panelists, run digital immersion sessions. When you speak to people individually or in small groups you can ask questions or hear specifics that underpin stories. Doing this reinforces the stories and lessons you learned. This is what it means to do digital.

To summarize, if we want to truly upskill people, we need to incentivize them to learn. Learning is an emotional investment. We have to stop pretending that error-proof web-based training teaches people anything. Why should I waste my time on cybersecurity training that will not increase my knowledge? This is disrespectful to the employee. We need to make the learning goal authentic and meaningful.[74] That motivation, matched with deep knowledge, will increase one's creativity and aptitude to solve complicated problems. These skills are what hackers embody. This is the approach we need to deliver to our supply chain professionals because this is how we will prepare for, improve, and secure our next-generation supply chains.

With these learning principles in mind, we can go about the task of creating new trainings that help us to learn digital by doing, much like the spear phishing example above. This means building entirely new curriculums and incentive structures. At a minimum, we can stop buying useless learning management systems (LMS)—this alone will save millions of dollars. I had one client tell me they spent $25 million on a new LMS. I almost fell out of my chair.

Hacking people: five takeaways

— Stop pretend-training and instead motivate employees to learn.

— Leaders need to eliminate the fear of failure and embrace it as part of the learning process.

— Create social learning experiences among teams both internally and externally.

— Maximize retention of new concepts and provide time to reflect.

— Allow employees to feel comfortable about not having all the answers.

[74] Brown et al. *Make It Stick*, 30.

Chapter VI
Hacking AI and building algorithmic literacy

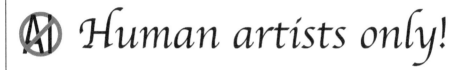

- Image generated by Dall-E-2

"[T]o really try to be informed and literate today is to feel stupid nearly all the time, and to need help."

– David Foster Wallace, The Best American Essays 2007

We've covered the basics of intelligence, tools, and people; the rapid evolution and advancement of AI will start to enhance each of those individual domains. This means supply chains will benefit from new ways of AI-generated intelligence and tools. However, we can't take advantage of these benefits until we better understand how these algorithms work.

Listen to any analyst, pundit, or consultant and they will continually reference algorithms. Every time I hear this word, it tickles the curiosity part of my brain. What or who is this algorithm? Is it a mathematical equation, is it an executable program, is it sentient, or is it something else? If it exists to improve operations (forecasting, routing, allocations) then who's in charge? Who understands the responsibility?

If we're going to build a next-generation supply chain, we need to grow a greater algorithmic literacy individually and within our teams. Increasingly, algorithms control our lives. If you use a smartphone, social media, e-commerce, take public transportation, drive a modern car, or have countless interactions with smart devices, you are encountering algorithms (a cynic might say we are manipulated by these algorithms). Algorithms are a crucial component of understanding AI. Thus, we need to understand how algorithms work, what they can and can't do, and how they can be manipulated. We must desensitize ourselves from the hype so that we can learn and use these very powerful tools. (See Figure 13: *The different types of AI* on page 91.)

I have three friends that are algorithms. I know that sounds weird and a tiny bit sad, but hear me out. I rely on my first friend, the YouTube algorithm, to teach me and build my intellectual curiosity by suggesting helpful videos. We tend to trust recommendations from our friends. In my case, some of my closest friends are mathematical (okay, that does sound sad). As we saw from my data tracking exercise above, I spend 30 minutes each day watching videos. I don't actually search for videos anymore. When I first started procrastinating on writing this book, I watched a few initial videos about Amazon Web Services, logistics in the Arctic, and the problems with corporate sustainability efforts. Since then, the algorithm has taken me on a wide and vast journey of recommendations that have helped me learn about the rise or fall of particular brands, how Amazon delivers packages to aircraft carriers deployed at sea, cybercrime, private equity, and all kinds of other random yet interesting and informative videos.[75] I have learned a tremendous amount of knowledge in a very short time simply by letting the YouTube recommendation engine learn a little about my interests—and yes, I do examine the content creators and validate their credentials as experts.

My next friend is the LinkedIn algorithm. As an influencer, I rely on it to promote me, to put my content into people's news feeds, and to recommend it to the proper people. It also gives me the latest news and activity about the people it thinks I need to know. This is a time multiplier for me.

---

[75] If you want to watch the videos you can find a playlist at https://www.drelouise.com/post/how-to-hack-your-supply-chain.

Figure 13
The different types of AI

 AI
Harnessing intelligent systems for human-like tasks

 Machine learning
Teaching systems to learn and improve on their own

 Deep learning
Autonomous self-learning

 Generative AI
Creating original content from input data

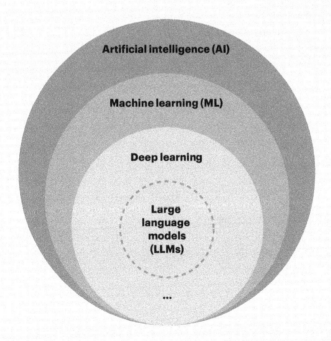

Source: Kearney

Finally, the Facebook algorithm talks to me. Don't worry, it's not a two-way conversation (that *would* be weird). When I transitioned, I deleted my old profile; it was anchored in anger and ego. Post transition, I created a new profile with only a handful of friends (78 as of this writing). I hardly post anything and rarely send messages. But I watch how every interaction influences the next. I add a Jewish friend and all of a sudden I get a whole series of recommended friends who are … you guessed it … Jewish. I click on a vegan ad and, guess what, I start to see all kinds of vegan ads in my feed. I watch a recommended inspirational video, and sure enough I see many more inspirational videos. As I interact with Facebook, the algorithm talks back with new and different content, suggestions, and recommendations. It is that response from the algorithm that intrigues me. You could say I am hacking these algorithms, but really I am simply reverse-engineering them to get what I want.

Chloé Zhao's film *Nomadland* explores the plight of itinerant older workers as they follow short-term employment throughout the year. Some of their work includes time in Amazon fulfillment centers as part of CamperForce, part of Amazon's seasonal hiring program for people who live in recreational vehicles.[76] What Zhao highlights is that for workers in these warehouses, their world is centered around handheld scanners. These scanners tell them what they need to do and where at any given time and, most importantly, how much time they have to complete the task. The managers have no control over what the employees are doing; the oversight comes from the nameless, faceless algorithm. In reality it is probably much more of a series of programmatically embedded algorithms within a custom software application (obviously, the mechanics are proprietary). The stark contrast between this algorithmic way of working and the past manager-centric control is worth noting. Since the advent of industrial operations, the manager has been responsible for what happens on the shop floor, ensuring the workers' productivity, the quality of the products, and the efficiency of the operations. What happens when the manager is no longer in charge, but instead a dislocated cog in relationship to the machine? As Zhao notes, the manager can have a caring relationship

---

[76] Part of the compensation included paying for RV campsite fees. Amazon recently discontinued the program as a standalone entity and wrapped it into its seasonal workforce management. Fedorick, Lynne. "Amazon CamperForce Discontinued." Camper Report, February 6, 2023. https://camperreport.com/amazon-camperforce-discontinued/ (Accessed May 11, 2023).

with the employee because the algorithm is the culprit or villain behind anything that goes wrong.[77]

In China, gig workers are directly confronting their algorithmic overlords. An estimated 200 million people work in the gig economy there. Increasingly, tech platforms have improved their algorithms to push workers to reduce delivery times to increase profits. Some of these changes include incorporating gamification so that workers are pitted against one another to compete for various statuses (bronze, silver, gold). The higher the achievement, the more take-home pay. Naturally, an increase in worker accidents and deaths has followed. In response, these workers have gamed the algorithm by banding together to share information and modify collective behavior. For example, using social media platforms like WeChat, workers will collectively reject orders for difficult areas, known as "no-fly zones," until orders come back with a higher price. They are hacking the way the algorithm operates to improve their working conditions. Workers will also create fake orders to improve their standing within the algorithm.[78]

How are we putting more faith and control into algorithmically controlled systems without fully understanding them? If this book were more of a social commentary, I might point out that algorithms used in policing rely on historical crime rates, location data, and demographic (socioeconomic background, education, and zip code) data to predict future crime. In the process, they perpetuate systematic racism because the data used to train these algorithms weights arrest rates higher than other factors and Black people are five times more likely to be arrested than white people. I might further point out that a predictive policing algorithm should weight conviction rates or severity of crime higher than arrest records. After all, being arrested for protesting at a Black Lives Matter rally is far different than defrauding the federal government of millions of dollars. The problem is that algorithms rely on statistics, which prioritize frequency, so the algorithm skews toward high frequency/low impact events (arrests) versus low frequency/high impact events (fraud convictions).[79] Alas, I digress once again.

[77] Bruder, Jessica. *Nomadland: Surviving America in the Twenty-First Century* (Farmington Hills, Michigan: Thorndike Press, 2018).
[78] Borak, Masha. "China's Gig Workers Are Challenging Algorithmic Bosses." Wired, March 14, 2022. https://www.wired.com/story/chinas-gig-workers-challenging-algorithmic-bosses/ (Accessed May 11, 2023).
[79] Heaven, Will Douglas. "Predictive policing algorithms are racist. They need to be dismantled." MIT Technology Review, July 17, 2020. https://www.technologyreview.com/2020/07/17/1005396/predictive-policing-algorithms-racist-dismantled-machine-learning-bias-criminal-justice/ (Accessed May 11, 2023).

We are rapidly entering a new phase in the digital era as China has started to regulate algorithms with its Provisions on the Management of Algorithmic Recommendations in Internet Information Services of March 1, 2022. Within these provisions, the Chinese government is forcing tech companies operating in China to be accountable for how their algorithms behave. According to the policy, the providers of algorithmic recommendation services:

— Must not set up algorithmic models that violate laws and regulations, or go against ethics and morals, such as by inducing users to become addicted or spend too much.

— Must not use algorithms to register fake accounts ... making excessive recommendations, manipulating the order of top content lists or search results, or controlling hot searches or selections, influencing online public opinion, or evading oversight and management.

— Must not use algorithms to unreasonably restrict other Internet information service providers, or to obstruct and undermine the normal operation of the Internet information services they lawfully provide, implementing a monopoly or unfair competition.

— Shall provide users with functions for selecting or deleting user labels used in algorithmic recommendation services that target their personal traits.

— Shall provide work coordination services for laborers; they shall protect the laborers' lawful rights and interests such as to receive salary and to rest and vacation, and establish and improve algorithms related to assigning orders, salary composition and payment, work times, rewards and penalties, and so forth.[80]

The EU and the UK are enacting similar legislation. This is a logical step as we have national and international systems to govern land, air, space, and water.

---

[80] "Provisions on the Management of Algorithmic Recommendations in Internet Information Services." China Law Translate. January 1, 2022. https://www.chinalawtranslate.com/en/algorithms/ (Accessed May 11, 2023).
Knight, Will. "China Wants to Regulate AI, but the World Should Be Wary." Wired, February 22, 2022. https://www.wired.com/story/china-regulate-ai-world-watching/ (Accessed May 11, 2023).

We are entering the phase where cyberspace is becoming regulated.[81] Case in point: America's Biden administration released an updated cybersecurity strategy proposal that will attempt to hold software companies liable for failing to put proper levels of security controls in their code.

As consumers and global citizens, we must take a much more active role in understanding how these systems work since increasingly they control (and manipulate) our lives. Algorithms shape how we shop, the media we consume, the news we ingest, how our retirement accounts are invested, and much more. Given the importance, programmers, engineers, and the companies that develop these algorithms need to be able to explain how they work to lawmakers, regulators, and the public. A loose understanding of how an algorithm came to an answer isn't enough.[82] So as we think about building the next-generation supply chain, one that at its core is driven by intelligent algorithms, we need a greater algorithmic literacy.

Machine learning: the basics

What if I told you that next-generation supply chains will be run using 12 algorithms? Would you agree, disagree, or counter? Do you have a guess? I don't actually know and, right now, nobody does, but that's the point. If we're going to talk about AI or algorithms in supply chains we'd better find out the answer—and pretty quick. Here's a brief non-technical primer on algorithms to start the exploration.

Please note there are classes, books, and undergraduate and graduate programs that study the discipline of machine learning and the related algorithms. What I am doing is providing the simplest definition so that we can collectively understand how all this "magic" works and apply it to building the future supply chain. Also, this is all changing very rapidly, and by the time this book goes to print it's likely there will be a new set of breakthroughs in this realm. Ultimately, if I get anything wrong, remember I'm a historian by training, not a mathematician or computer scientist.

---

[81] Sanger, David W. "Biden Unveils Ambitious Cybersecurity Strategy." The New York Times, March 2, 2023. https://www.nytimes.com/2023/03/02/us/politics/biden-cybersecurity-strategy.html (Accessed May 11, 2023).
[82] Cascio, Jamais. "Facing the Age of Chaos." Medium (Accessed April 29, 2020). https://medium.com/@cascio/facing-the-age-of-chaos-b00687b1f51d (Accessed May 11, 2023).

According to computer scientist Hilary Mason, machine learning teaches computers to recognize and learn patterns from data and apply them to new things they haven't seen before. This is accomplished through an algorithm, which is a set of steps that takes input data, processes it, and outputs new data.[83] In succinct terms, machines are good at detecting patterns. For example, they are particularly good at looking at historical patterns to predict the future. This is called regression and is often used in forecasting and demand-planning activities.

Under the machine learning umbrella, there are seven basic concepts to understand (and if this is the only takeaway from this chapter, then that should be a win). Also, none of these is mutually exclusive; algorithms are frequently combined with one another, especially the last one.

— **Data label.** This is where we describe raw data to provide the algorithm context for what the data is.

— **Model.** This is the output of an algorithm run on data.

— **Supervised learning (SL).** This is where we have a labeled data set with the answers and we train the model to determine what is statistically significant. This is often used for forecasting and predicting future actions through regression analysis.

— **Unsupervised learning (UL).** We don't have labels for the data so we are using the algorithms to infer structure and labels out of the data by identifying clusters of data.

[83] "Algorithm." Dictionary.com. https://www.dictionary.com/browse/algorithm (Accessed May 11, 2023).
Wired. "Computer Scientist Explains Machine Learning in 5 Levels of Difficulty." YouTube video, 25:54. August 18, 2021. https://www.youtube.com/watch?v=5q87K1WaoFI (Accessed May 11, 2023).
Upadhyay, Soni. "What is an Algorithm?" Simplilearn. February 21, 2023. https://www.simplilearn.com/tutorials/data-structure-tutorial/what-is-an-algorithm (Accessed May 11, 2023).
"Neural Network." Amazon Web Services (AWS). https://aws.amazon.com/what-is/neural-network/ (Accessed May 11, 2023).
Bhatt, Shweta. "Reinforcement Learning 101." Towards Data Science, March 19, 2018. https://towardsdatascience.com/reinforcement-learning-101-e24b50e1d292 (Accessed May 11, 2023).
Bajaj, Prateek. "What is Reinforcement Learning?" GeeksforGeeks. https://www.geeksforgeeks.org/what-is-reinforcement-learning/ (Accessed May 11, 2023).
Rouse, Margaret. "Deep Reinforcement Learning (Deep RL)." Techopedia. June 28, 2022. https://www.techopedia.com/definition/34029/deep-reinforcement-learning-deep-rl (Accessed May 11, 2023).

— **Reinforcement learning (RL).** This is an autonomous, self-learning method that uses trial and error to learn from experience. Think of a Roomba that learns the layout of a room by simply mapping where the objects are located by bumping into them.

— **Neural network (NN).** This is a machine learning method to process data as the human brain would. It uses interconnected algorithmic structures (like neurons in a brain) to employ multiple models to learn and model complex data input and output.

— **Deep learning (DL).** This is an autonomous self-learning method, using neural networks, that employs an existing large data set for training before it's applied to predict new data. Think of facial recognition on an iPhone that maps your face (training data) and when you use your face to log in, it predicts whether you are you.

— **Deep reinforcement learning (DRL).** As the name suggests, this is a combination of deep learning and reinforcement learning. This is where a neural network learns through trial and error. DRL is used in autonomous vehicles. As you can probably imagine, this gets extraordinarily technical quickly.

In case you're wondering, the wildly popular ChatGPT makes use of a newer deep learning model known as transformers. Historically, when training a model to understand a sentence, the model analyzes text word by word. Now transformers can process an entire sentence at once, making them far more efficient to train. It also makes use of large language models (LLM), part of natural language processing. LLMs are a sophisticated way to process and infer the relationships between words in enormously large amounts of text.[84]

[84] Greengard, Samuel. "ChatGPT: Understanding the ChatGPT AI Chatbot." eWeek. December 29, 2022. https://www.eweek.com/big-data-and-analytics/chatgpt/ (Accessed May 11, 2023).
Ruby, Molly "How ChatGPT Works: The Models Behind the Bot." Towards Data Science, January 30, 2023. https://medium.com/towards-data-science/how-chatgpt-works-the-models-behind-the-bot-1ce5fca96286 (Accessed May 11, 2023).

But how does this affect supply chains?

At this point I know you're thinking, "Enough of the jargon, get to the point." How do we apply all this fancy machine learning to supply chain problems? Each of these concepts is already used in supply chain management. Supervised learning is used for demand forecasting, spend data classification, fraud detection, and (my personal favorite) data management. Unsupervised learning is used for market basket analysis, contract analytics (think clustering of clauses), and logistics optimization. Deep reinforcement learning is used with robots on manufacturing production lines and in logistics centers (transporting, picking, packing, palletizing/depalletizing); we are well into the machine learning for supply chain journey.

For us to truly build the next-generation AI supply chain we need to understand how to better make use of these algorithms and ensure they aren't directed against us. First, we need this level of understanding so that you can make better buying decisions when solution providers, consultants, and contractors try to sell you "AI and machine learning." Here is an excerpt from a spam message I received while writing this chapter:

"To stay ahead of the curve, procurement teams must adopt a more innovative approach. They need to move toward the use of AI and machine learning to plot the complex variables involved in supply chain planning."

Naturally, I am skeptical, if not downright dismissive, of statements like these. I want every supply chain professional to not only view these messages with the same level of skepticism but also to be able to challenge back and ask them what kind of DL or RDL they use. This is the technique I use because it quickly separates the posers from those who know what they're doing. The posers will start spewing out more jargon. Those who understand machine learning will stop and clarify what they're doing (supervised and unsupervised versus RL/DL/RDL). The fact is that RL/DL/RDL all take significant amounts of data to be relevant (think mapping the human genome), which is way more data than most start-ups have.

As you can see from the RL, DL, and RDL algorithms, they learn and act autonomously based on the data they ingest and how they interpret it. When there are multiple layers of data interpretation based on historical learning and data modeling, it can be nearly impossible to explain why two outcomes might be different. In other words, no core set of rules explains a particular action. A good example of this is Google Search's autofill feature, which may offer you and your colleague across the globe different autofill responses. Naturally, this is going to make it difficult to comply with legislation. Regarding third parties, this lack of standard rules begs some difficult contractual questions. If an enterprise uses a solution that gets smarter because of the data provided by the enterprise, is it entitled to compensation because it made the algorithm and, thus, the solution better? What happens when you stop using the solution? Moreover, who is liable if the solution makes a costly mistake?

The most important reason to learn how machine learning algorithms work is so you can understand how they can be hacked. As explained above, when Chinese tech companies put gamification into the gig worker apps, workers gamed the system by putting in fake orders. This happens all the time on review sites and search engine optimization. If you want to sell a product and displace your competitor online, you don't need a better product or a lower price, you simply need to trick the search algorithm into prioritizing your goods over your competitors'. In other words, data can be used to manipulate algorithms. We must appreciate this fact before implementing algorithms everywhere in our supply chains.

Consider how many user consumption forecasting models will be skewed because of the pandemic. Look at historical data trends of airline travel, toilet paper, car purchases, and technology purchases—all were skewed by the pandemic. If you study the consumption data of any of these over the past five years, it will look very strange for 2020 and 2021 (and possibly 2022). So how do you predict what will happen in 2023, 2024, and beyond? Every leader must understand and wrestle with these questions. The point here is not to solve that problem but rather to reinforce the importance of data cleanliness and governance. The observant reader will rightly have deduced from the algorithm explanation above that machine learning can also be applied to data management with significant success. This is a whole discipline in itself (see my spider map on LinkedIn for some companies that do this). However, it also means there is no excuse for bad data or a lack of data governance.

How to learn more

I recommend playing with algorithms. Create a temporary social media or e-commerce account and watch how the algorithm customizes itself to you. Observe how it changes what you see based on how you interact. Even better, do the same exercise with a friend so you can engage in social-based learning. Or spend some time with ChatGPT and see if you can jailbreak it by circumventing its editorial controls.[85] Engage with Siri/Google/Alexa and see how you can use algorithms to hack your daily routine and squeeze out more personal free time.

Hacking AI: five takeaways

— Make friends with the algorithms in your life.

— Explore the basics of machine learning.

— Predict the 12 algorithms that will run future supply chains.

— Study the impact regulations will have on using algorithms.

— Put learning AI at the top of your to-do list.

[85] King, Michael. "Upgraded Dan Version for ChatGPT is Here: New, Shiny, and More Unchained." Neon Forge (Accessed February 10, 2023) . https://medium.com/@neonforge/upgraded-dan-version-for-chatgpt-is-here-new-shiny-and-more-unchained-63d82919d804 (Accessed May 11, 2023).

Chapter VII
Hacking resilience: how quickly can your supply chain recover?

"Most companies wait for the boom to happen and then respond."

– Johan Gott, co-founder of PRISM advisory risk company

"Detection is useless without response."

– Bruce Schneier, renowned computer security expert and author

Once we have secured the individual parts of our supply chain we can start to build resilience— the ability to recover from disruption. At this point it's natural to focus on the *why*—that's the most interesting part. It's easy to explain why supply chains are broken, but building resilience is significantly harder because we have to get into the details of what is broken and try to fix it. Sometimes these fixes require unwinding decades of investment and ineffective strategies. Often, resilience return on investment is fleeting and becomes more of an insurance policy than a strategic initiative. Regardless, it's time to move resilience conversations beyond why it's important and toward making our supply chains more fault tolerant.

10-word answers

Many days, I wake up, open LinkedIn, scroll through my feed, and think, "For goodness' sake, I really hate consultants." The irony of my statement notwithstanding, consultants are very smart people, but oftentimes they fall into professional groupthink, not only among individual firms but also across the entire profession. This can be clearly seen in the topic of resilience.

Coming out of the pandemic, every firm developed a perspective on building resilience in the supply chain. Without singling out any firm, if you read the various perspectives from Accenture, Bain, BCG, Deloitte, Kearney, and McKinsey, you'll come away with the following messages:

— Resilience is important; act now.

— Take a resilience stress test.

— Do better planning and adjust your sourcing strategy.

— Move/reposition your manufacturing sites.

— Create a resilient network design.

All of these are great suggestions, and they look good on glossy brochures, in white papers, or in slick PowerPoint decks, but they mean very little in practical terms. They are deliberately broad and lack practical applicability.

The West Wing fans will be struck by the "10-word answers" phenomenon as seen in season four, episode six.[86] During the episode, there is a presidential debate between fictional president Jed Bartlet, played by Martin Sheen (and meant to represent an idealized version of a liberal intellectual Democrat), and Florida governor Robert Ritchie, played by James Brolin (meant to be a slick-talking, America-loving conservative, and a not-so-subtle jab at then-US President George W. Bush). During the debate, the following exchange takes place:

Moderator: *Governor Ritchie, many economists have stated that the tax cut, which is the centerpiece of your economic agenda, could harm the economy. Is now really the time to cut taxes?*

Governor Robert Ritchie, R-FL: *You bet it is. We need to cut taxes for one reason—the American people know how to spend their money better than the federal government does.*

[86] "Game On." *The West Wing,* season four, episode six, aired October 30, 2002.

Moderator: *Mr. President, your rebuttal.*

President Bartlet: *There it is. That's the 10-word answer my staff's been looking for for two weeks. There it is. Ten-word answers can kill you in political campaigns. They're the tip of the sword. Here's my question: what are the next 10 words of your answer? Your taxes are too high? So are mine. Give me the next 10 words. How are we going to do it? Give me 10 after that, I'll drop out of the race right now.*

President Bartlet explains that governing is messy, difficult, and that determining right from wrong in the real world is hard. The point of this exchange is to show that it is easy to give a slick 10-word answer, but to get the work done in a high-pressure, volatile, politically contentious environment is difficult. I think it would be fair to use this construct to describe the way building resilience is portrayed by analysts, consultants, and pundits in real-world supply chains.

If you read what industry analysts, consultants, and solution providers offer up, it is some variant of a three- or five-point plan (the equivalent of a 10-word answer). Again, combining the answers from all the firms, one gets a picture that resilience requires some combination of:

— People

— Process

— Tools

— Culture

— Governance

— Change management

— Data and analytics

In other words, the consulting profession's answer to resilience is to create a new and better op model. Pardon me if I am underwhelmed because redoing the op model seems to be the consultant's answer to just about every business problem. We can debate the efficacy of op model designs and redesigns on business problems writ large (perhaps in my next book about the consulting profession). However, what's undeniable is that building a resilient supply chain will take more than 10-word answers or op model designs in PowerPoint. Moreover, many of the recommendations look great on paper, such as, "Don't single source" or "Move manufacturing locations near/onshore." Great in theory and in boardrooms, but far more difficult in practical terms. More importantly, this does not make any enterprise more resilient.

More maddening is the bevy of suggestions that call for some combination of creating network visibility, KPIs, real-time monitoring, predictive modeling, playbooks, and the like. Then there are the suggestions to integrate resilience into every supply chain function while building "strategic, tactical, analytical, and digital" talent. But my favorite is creating a culture of resilience by "winning the hearts and minds of employees." I want to print out all these white papers, bind them into a book, then burn them as an effigy to excise the demons of mediocrity. Recognizing that I would be perpetuating several levels of environmental damage by doing that, I will simply take the downloaded PDFs of these "resilience playbooks," drag them into the trash on my computer, and empty it. With those demons excised, we can now get to the task of building resilient supply chains. The first order of business is to get good at risk management. (See sidebar: *Tyranny of the obvious: five-point plans* on page 105.)

Tyranny of the obvious: five-point plans

I have created random five-point plans from all the white papers. These are mixed from multiple publications. Perhaps it's not fair that I took them out of context. However, each of these recommendations seems extraordinarily obvious. I wonder if the authors could even pick out their recommendations from others. Maybe the better question is, could ChatGPT come up with the same answer?

Random five-point plan #1

1. Optimize inventory.

2. Embed intelligence to learn from buying patterns.

3. Add distribution partners.

4. Increase capabilities.

5. Identify and classify third parties.

Random five-point plan #2

1. Embed AI into procurement platforms.

2. Design and implement a robust supplier security management strategy and processes.

3. Exploit data and emerging technologies.

4. Build resilience to absorb and avoid disruptions.

5. Use predictive analytics based on previous events.

(continued on next page)

Tyranny of the obvious: five-point plans (continued)

Random five-point plan #3

1. React to threats and disruptions.

2. Mitigate risks proactively with prescriptive analytics. Build end-to-end capabilities.

3. Convince suppliers to shift production.

4. Qualify back-up contract manufacturers.

5. Design and implement solutions that help alleviate vulnerabilities.

Random five-point plan #4

1. Reshore/regionalize.

2. Optimize raw material inventory.

3. Reallocate sourcing among supplier locations.

4. Qualify new suppliers.

5. Utilize multi-tier data sharing and collaboration.

Random five-point plan #5

1. Improve processes in planning, sourcing, production, and distribution (this wins the award for the most useless recommendation).

2. Reduce risk to an acceptable level.

3. Drive leadership accountability.

4. Encourage learning communities.

5. Create visibility into the extended supply chain.

Living in a FUD, VUCA, BANI world

I am on record as hating lazy consulting. Perhaps the most egregious example of lazy consulting is the pushing of fear. This is not limited to consultants alone, but also solution providers, analysts, pundits and the like who espouse fear-based narratives. This explains why we have various frameworks for dealing with the chaotic nature of the world. First up is fear, uncertainty, and doubt (FUD), which is common in security. There is volatility, uncertainty, complexity, and ambiguity (VUCA), which traces its lineage to the US Army War College in the late 1980s. Now there is brittle, anxious, nonlinear, and incomprehensible (BANI).[87] This alphabet soup of acronyms is enough to stoke the fires of angst, panic, and concern. However, generating fear based on society's collective anxieties and traumas simply to sell software and services seems opportunistic at best and pernicious (if not unethical) at worst. And yet this is the lifeblood of the risk management space (and the others who provide solutions and services). The more FUD/VUCA/BANI we create, the more clients feel like they need us. If you don't believe me, download the oceans of white papers or LinkedIn posts put out by consulting firms. The entire security industry is built on this paradigm. One of the most eye-rolling calls I endured was listening to a bunch of consultants getting on the phone as part of an exercise to predict the big disruption—so they could develop a solution around it before it even happened. The entire exercise was meant to identify a FUD/VUCA/BANI issue and peddle it with a corollary solution. Needless to say, I displayed less than collegial behavior.

Jamais Cascio, co-creator of the BANI framework, criticizes VUCA as "simply a depiction of our default condition ... declaring a situation or a system to be volatile or ambiguous tells us nothing new." This is why all those white papers read like visual white noise. It is worth noting that Cascio and his collaborators shift the discussion to four new concepts: brittle, anxious, nonlinear, and incomprehensible. These terms do a better job of describing why our current

---

[87] Turns out there are also rapid, unpredictable, paradoxical, tangled (RUPT) and turbulent, uncertain, novel, ambiguous (TUNA) frameworks too.
Cascio, Jamais. "Facing the Age of Chaos." Medium, April 29, 2020. https://medium.com/@cascio/facing-the-age-of-chaos-b00687b1f51d (Accessed May 11, 2023).
VUCA-World. "Vuca Bani Rupt Tuna." VUCA Blog. https://www.vuca-world.org/vuca-bani-rupt-tuna/ (Accessed May 11, 2023).

supply chains are broken. For example, the BANI creators define the B as "[a] brittle system in a BANI world [that] may be signaling all along that it's good, it's strong, it's able to continue, even as it's on the precipice of collapse. Brittle systems do not fail gracefully; they shatter. Brittleness often arises from efforts to maximize efficiency, to wring every last bit of value—money, power, food, work—from a system."[88] However, as good as it is as a descriptor, BANI (like FUD and VUCA) do little more than to explain the lack of resilience in our supply chain designs because of the vast complexity in moving supply chains across the entire globe.

To see a great example of just how complicated today's supply chains are, look no further than Christopher Mims' book *Arriving Today: From Factory to Front Door—Why Everything Has Changed About How and What We Buy*. He tracks a hypothetical USB charger on its journey from the docks of Vietnam to its final destination at a house in the US state of Connecticut. Through the illustration of the USB charger's journey, Mims explores container ships, containers, port operations, Amazon, UPS, interstate trucking, and last-mile delivery. It's an incredibly poignant and illuminating mapping of today's global supply chains. Though not his stated intention, his book shows just how brittle supply chains are and how easily disrupted they can be. More to the point, there are so many third parties involved and handoffs between them that it is clear every supply chain is a soft target waiting to be hacked, stolen, or disrupted.

Ultimately, it doesn't matter to me which framework you choose—or if you even use one. The key takeaway is that the frameworks explain *why* our supply chains (and perhaps the world) are continually in crisis. But they lack the *how* we fix it aspect. Therefore, I would like to offer a perspective on how we fix them. To do that, looking at the disaster management space and using at least one of their frameworks is useful.

The boom framework

All the purported resilience frameworks, op models, and PowerPoints are focused on the idea that if you pull a set of levers, you can withstand any

---

[88] Cascio, Jamais. "Facing the Age of Chaos." Medium, April 29, 2020. https://medium.com/@cascio/facing-the-age-of-chaos-b00687b1f51d (Accessed May 11, 2023).

disruption. They also assume that there is a steady state of operations, then a disruption must be absorbed and acted upon. Afterward, things go back to a steady state. Unfortunately, that is not the world we live in anymore. If we want to talk about resilience from a practical point of view, there is plenty of great real-world experience and material we can use from the disaster management domain. Juliette Kayyem's *The Devil Never Sleeps* lays out a useful framework for disaster management. She and other disaster planners use the concept of the boom, which represents the disaster itself. She argues that the boom is inevitable. So disaster management work is left-of-boom: avoiding the disaster or minimizing the damage. And the right-of-boom activities are what we do in response to the disruption.[89] (See Figure 14: *The boom framework.*)

[89] Kayyem, Juliette. *The Devil Never Sleeps: Learning to Live in an Age of Disasters* (New York: PublicAffairs, 2022) Hardcover – March 29, 2022.

Figure 14
The boom framework

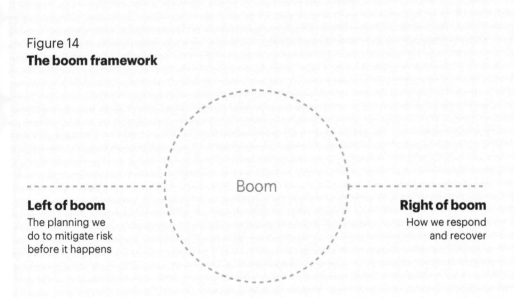

Left of boom
The planning we
do to mitigate risk
before it happens

Boom

Right of boom
How we respond
and recover

Source: Kayyem, Juliette. *The Devil Never Sleeps: Learning to Live in an Age of Disasters* (New York: Hachette Book Group Inc., 2022). March 29, 2022.

The boom approach is useful if we're going to build resilient supply chains. If we assume the boom is continual, as Kayyem eloquently describes, "[f]or there to be a start, it assumes a finish ... For you to stop worrying, it assumes there was a time of unicorns and rainbows when days were carefree and weightless. I'm here to disabuse you of that notion. There is no finish line."[90] To build true resilience, we must categorize our activities into left and right of boom. What investments (for example, digital solutions and people capabilities) and planning (network design/redesign, stockpiling, sourcing) can we tackle before a boom occurs? For right of boom, what procedures do we have in place to react in a nimble way? Do we have real-time visibility as events unfold? Can we quickly enact or model alternate scenarios? How quickly can we switch supply sources or distribution networks? Readers may notice that some of these recommendations are the same as the laundry list of "resilience five-point plans." The ideas are relevant, but they lacked the context and the how, which is what follows.

According to Kayyem, "Disaster management is about being ready for any boom in any shape. This concept, known as all-hazards planning, does not focus on one specific hazard but instead on all of them."[91] This is crucial in designing and building the next-generation supply chain.

Left of boom: how we prepare

Left of boom is the planning we do to mitigate risk before it happens. To do this we must build a strong situational analysis of our supply chains. This is where the hacking mindset comes in—we need to stop and take a critical look at our end-to-end supply chains and imagine where they may be attacked and how. Essentially, we want to break down our supply chains to their core components to rebuild them more securely. We have these functional silos of plan, source, make, and deliver, but as with any silo, we tend to hoard data and intelligence, which prevents us from seeing the total picture. When it comes to cyberthreats across thousands of third parties, the hoarding of information in silos gives an unfair advantage to the adversary. Going back to the vaccine example at the beginning, think about all the information silos and the various

---

[90] Kayyem, *The Devil Never Sleeps*, 17.
[91] Kayyem, *The Devil Never Sleeps*, 18.

handoffs. All an attacker needs to do is to insert an attack (physical or cyber) at any stage and it will carry through undetected the rest of the way.

A key question to look at in left-of-boom planning is how are we applying lessons learned from the past? What are the known risks we have encountered before? This includes risks that companies regularly face such as inflation, political instability, and supply shortages—to name just a few. Companies have strategies for addressing these (we hope) and can enact them once they occur. Then there are the emerging risks—events that you should be looking into but currently are not. A good example of this is industrial control systems (ICS). If you have responsibility for any third party that relies heavily on ICS, you should be very worried. There have been two very high-profile successful attacks on industrial control systems—the same controllers your third parties use. Iran's nuclear centrifuges were attacked by software worms (the Stuxnet worm) that were introduced into the ICS to force the centrifuges to break. In 2016, Russia took down Ukraine's power grid, using an Industroyer tool to thrust Kyiv into darkness.[92]

Both these examples were state-sponsored acts of aggression. However, the same tools deployed could be pointed at any industrial control system. Industrial control systems are notoriously insecure, and yet few risk managers, CIOs, category/commodity managers, and supply chain leaders are examining the weaknesses and making them more secure.

Indirect suppliers can cause similar catastrophes. The SaaS solutions that many businesses rely on also introduce risk. For example, I had a client confide in me that they put a significant operational capability—along with the related customer data—into a SaaS provider. The company did all the upfront due diligence, security questionnaires, and quarterly and annual business reviews. In short, the decision-makers performed the risk theater as well as actors performing a Broadway play. Then the tech company decided to shut down with only 60 days' notice. The enterprise had to make a multimillion-dollar investment to shore up the SaaS company so that the business could buy enough time to figure out an alternative plan.

---

[92] Perlroth, Nicole. *This Is How They Tell Me the World Ends: The Cyberweapons Arms Race* (New York: Bloomsbury Publishing, 2021).
Zetter, Kim. *Countdown to Zero Day: Stuxnet and the Launch of the World's First Digital Weapon* (New York: Random House, LLC, 2014).

Sadly, this is a common experience. In fact, a consulting firm I am intimately familiar with had exactly the same issue. The natural reaction is to say, "Don't use start-up SaaS platforms," but of course that doesn't work either. The breakdown was that everyone communicated that everything was great until it wasn't. This is why we need to take a critical look at these relationships and find the points of vulnerability; we need to know what we don't know. Going further, enterprises must prepare for the boom across the entire supply chain ecosystem of third parties. It's not about the single threat but how any threat can disrupt our operations. You can't focus on cybersecurity while ignoring physical security. We must look at who is attacking, what are they trying to get, and what's the probability and likelihood of an attack.[93] This is why left-of-boom preparation requires a holistic view of the risk of third parties.

Ultimately, left-of-boom preparation is a financial decision. How much money does an enterprise want to spend defending itself against potential attackers? We must weigh the trade-off of a risk between a disruption versus forcing the company out of business. Supply risk can be mitigated by simply stockpiling key components. This approach can be expensive but can create a competitive advantage if you are the only one able to deliver in a constrained market. Similarly, companies will hedge commodity prices as a way of offsetting price fluctuations. Stockpiling and hedging are left-of-boom activities that mitigate known risks.

Here's a quick guide (adapted from security methodologies):[94]

1. Who are our third parties, and what risk do they pose, directly or indirectly?

2. What are the possible threat vectors?

3. What is the efficacy of the security controls we have in place?

4. What collateral damage could a disruption to this third party cause?

5. What are we not doing that we should be doing?

---

[93] Schneier, Bruce. *Beyond Fear: Thinking Sensibly About Security in an Uncertain World* (New York: Copernicus Books, 2006), 83.
[94] Schneier, *Beyond Fear*, 14-15.

To answer any of these questions, you must have someone (or a team) who is incentivized to care. If not, there is nobody with ultimate responsibility and third-party risk mitigation becomes a matter of luck. Equally important in answering these questions is knowing who your third parties are and why they are in your system. In our complicated business environment of third parties, today's supplier is tomorrow's competitor or unwitting attacker. For example, your suppliers may be customers, or your customers may be competitor frenemies. This is why data mastery of your third-party entities is so crucial.

Data can be overwhelming, but it doesn't have to be. My data collection and governance example in the previous chapter seems so simple. But it's not exceedingly more difficult to do it for the enterprise. And the importance of strong data management simply cannot be overstated. Data is the lifeblood of left-of-boom preparation activities. Our ability to collect, process, and analyze third-party data helps us to better manage our third parties. And better management of our third parties improves our risk management posture. The real risk here is overcomplicating third-party data management to such a degree that we cannot effectively do left-of-boom planning.

Right of boom: how we respond

Right of boom is the work we do to respond to and recover from the disaster once it occurs.[95] What good is it to have all the fancy risk-monitoring tools if nobody is looking at them? I have watched clients buy risk tool after risk tool only to watch them collect proverbial dust on a shelf. Yes, there are pretty dashboards created for review meetings and annual performance reviews, but what about daily operations? How are we applying the risk data to management? The even more important question is: What do we do with the data, especially when attacks are infrequent? Defenders have to be perfect 100 percent of the time; attackers only need to get it right once, which is why risk is a collective endeavor. You may not be attacked today, but your competitor, strategic partner, or supplier might be. The natural response to perceived threats is to create change management and communication plans. On the surface, there's nothing wrong with these. We need to know what to do, whom to communicate with, and how to communicate during a risk event.

---

[95] Kayyem, *The Devil Never Sleeps*, 19.

However, these management plans often become a means to their own end. They exist simply to justify the resources to create them. How many middle managers justify their existence by creating resilience plans? Or worse, they hire consultants to develop resilience plans that will never leave the safe confines of a PowerPoint slide.

If the disaster response plan is not operational, tested, and lived, it is simply a suggestion. Here's a good guide, again adapted from the security profession:[96]

1. **Decide who responds.** When hackers breach a system, who cuts off their access? Who does this when it is a supplier?

2. **Determine the responses.** What do you do when the boom hits? Consider how you'll marshal forces to protect the enterprise and ensure that you're not paying a fraudulent supplier.

3. **Plan for recovery.** How do you activate new capacity when the plant burns to the ground? What additional capacity do you have?

4. **Understand past lessons.** What can you do today to ensure that it doesn't happen again? For example, how do you ensure the FedEx delivery person is legitimate and not there to hack your keycard scanners?

5. **Use your experience to improve your defense.** Where can you share your experience more broadly with peers so that the industry can increase its collective defense? Also, consider reporting the attack to governmental authorities so that they can extract retribution. If companies never report breaches, these attacks will continue.

With the proper underlying cloud infrastructure, tools, intelligence, and people capability, we can operationalize disaster response into our daily working. As a matter of course, we can continually change our supply allocations to test the ability of one supplier to ramp up capacity. And we can proactively add more supplier capacity into our allocations. Some enterprises already do this to achieve cost savings for certain commodities (changing formulations

---

[96] Schneier, *Beyond Fear*, 167.

based on commodity prices). This needs to be expanded to the rest of the supply chain. Most importantly, we need to be able to make these changes with the push of a button—automate systems to do so as AI gets more sophisticated. Even better, companies should invite third parties (especially suppliers) into the conversation. Reach out to suppliers with outlier behavior profiles and talk to them about it. If we don't know details about supplier activity, we need to correct that—and soon.

Additionally, we should be continually attacking our systems to see where they are vulnerable. Hire college interns to try to break into your systems. Have them see if they can insert fake suppliers into your payment systems. In other words, *make it real*. Take 10 percent of everyone's job and have them study and share new physical or cyberattack profiles. Or once a month have the entire team create hacking scenarios and test them out. Create a hacking KPI to track found vulnerabilities. Use social learning to expand everyone's situational awareness. Start meetings by asking how many suppliers are in the system on any given day, what's the last login, what supplier has the longest duration since they logged into a system, or what supplier is an outlier behaviorally. These are questions that help daily operations, but they also give you a leg up on disaster response because it is testing the same skills that will be required when the boom hits. (See sidebar: *Why wars are not supply chain disruptions* on page 116.)

Hacking resilience: five takeaways

— Avoid 10-word answers to resilience.

— Building resilience requires a cultural shift.

— Left of boom is the planning we do to mitigate risk before it happens.

— Right of boom is how we respond and recover.

— We should be continually attacking our systems to make them stronger.

Why wars are not supply chain disruptions

When Russia invaded Ukraine in February 2022, the supply chain hype machine spun into action to talk about how this war was the next disruption. However, suggesting that the war is merely a supply chain disruption is a vast oversimplification. Ever since Russia's incursion into Ukraine, thousands upon thousands of people have been killed, tens of thousands injured or maimed, and hundreds of thousands forced to suffer incalculable hardships.

This is to say nothing of the untold environmental damage exacted upon the earth, so it is a little disingenuous to simply talk about the impact of the Ukraine war on enterprise supply chains. It's a matter of perspective. Supply chain solution providers have thrown the Ukraine war around as proof positive to build resilient supply chains. While technically correct, it misses the broader context and diminishes the much larger consequences of war. Wars are armed conflicts. They reshape entire societies and alter the course of history. So while the Ukraine war has caused energy prices to spike and diminished the availability of fertilizer, among other hardships, please keep in mind that these are small problems compared to the pain and suffering, the direct effects of trying to stay alive in a war zone.

Chapter VIII
Risk management: the bridge between security and resilience

"Time is what determines security. With enough time nothing is unhackable."

– Aniekee Tochukwu Ezekiel

There is a lot of confusion between security, risk management, and resilience. These terms are often used interchangeably, creating confusion. The concepts are related, but distinctly different. Security is the act of protecting something; resilience is the ability to recover from disruption. Risk management bridges the two by managing all the security efforts by using intelligence, tools, and people to create a strategy and protect the entire supply chain. In the process, this increases operational resilience. Doing effective risk management is hard; it requires a wide-ranging set of capabilities and an understanding of the pitfalls.

When's the best time to rob a bank?

Bank robber extraordinaire Daniel Blanchard answered this question on a Saturday morning in May 2004 when he walked up to a branch of the Canadian Imperial Bank of Commerce and stole nearly half a million dollars in cash. The money was delivered to the bank hours earlier in preparation for a Monday grand opening. Blanchard developed a very thorough and precise robbery technique that included doing significant amounts of surveillance during the construction process. "As the bank was being built, Blanchard frequently sneaked inside ... disguised as a delivery person or construction worker ... that allowed Blanchard to plant various surveillance devices in the ATM room. He knew when the cash machines were installed and what kind of locks they had. He ordered the same locks online and reverse engineered them at home."[97] Armed with this intelligence, he was able to rob the ATMs and leave the crime scene so intact that when the Winnipeg Police Service showed up (eight minutes after the alarm sounded), they concluded that it was a false alarm.

As a further cautionary tale, Blanchard had installed his own surveillance equipment inside the bank, allowing him to listen in as investigators conducted their investigation. Then he pretended to be an anonymous tipster and submitted bogus leads to keep detectives off his trail. This crime would have been unsolved had it not been for a Walmart associate (Walmart and the bank shared the same parking lot) who noted the license plate of Blanchard's minivan and gave it to the police. They eventually caught him.

Blanchard's successful robbery demonstrated exquisite use of intelligence, tools, and people. He highlighted some serious physical security flaws. He described showing up to bank construction sites "in broad daylight, disguised as a delivery person or construction worker … [s]ometimes it was just a matter of donning a yellow hard hat from Home Depot … [he] procured and stockpiled IDs and uniforms from various security companies and even law enforcement agencies."

The bank robber also identified some serious operational design flaws. Through his unfettered intelligence gathering, he deduced that security is more lax before the money shows up. Security during construction is focused on preventing materials from being stolen from the site rather than restricting access.[98] He also realized that many banks used Mas-Hamilton or La Gard locks. Naturally, Blanchard acquired his own, teaching himself to assemble and disassemble them in 40 seconds.

[97] Bearman, Joshuah. "Art of the Steal: On the Trail of the World's Most Ingenious Thief." Wired. March 22, 2010. https://www.wired.com/2010/03/ff-masterthief-blanchard/ (Accessed May 11, 2023).
[98] Bearman, Joshuah. "Art of the Steal: On the Trail of the World's Most Ingenious Thief." Wired. March 22, 2010. https://www.wired.com/2010/03/ff-masterthief-blanchard/ (Accessed May 11, 2023). "Historical Weather on Saturday, May 15, 2004 at Winnipeg (The Forks), Man., Canada." WeatherSpark. https://weatherspark.com/h/d/145966/2004/5/15/Historical-Weather-on-Saturday-May-15-2004-at-Winnipeg-The-Forks-Man.;-Canada#Figures-Temperature (Accessed May 11, 2023).

This story shines a light on the weakness of physical security. Interestingly, I have driven up to a client's physical security barrier and noted that "I'm here to see Brian Smith," the name of my client. That's all it takes to get into the facility. I couldn't pick a more generic name—it's almost too obvious. What's more concerning is that in a sleep-deprived state I once gave the wrong name, "John Smith," and the barrier opened without so much as a second glance from security. In Blanchard's example, we also discover just how easy it is to access a building with only a uniform. What authority does a UPS or FedEx uniform convey? How often do we simply look past the hundreds of Uber/Lyft/DoorDash delivery folks making their way in and out of corporate campuses? How many buildings can I get into by simply donning an Amazon vest, available for $20 on eBay?[99]

Blanchard didn't hack just a few Canadian banks; he hacked the entire ATM supply chain, not to mention parts of the police investigations. He developed a comprehensive and sophisticated understanding of the process, operations, technology, and security surrounding the building and deployment of banks and ATMs. Had he not been caught (by a fluke), there's no telling how many more banks he would have robbed.

My presumption is that the ATM supply chain was vastly overhauled once Blanchard's crimes were exposed. But what can we learn from this? First, it is the perfect example of using identity theft protection. This robbery occurred because of Blanchard's intelligence collection. Second, Blanchard made exceptional use of tools (locks, outfits, surveillance equipment). Finally, the people in charge of protection made a whole series of assumptions (what security guards were or were not protecting, that locks will keep people out, that physical security was sufficient) that Blanchard exploited. Taken together, the story illustrated the need to understand when and where risk is likely to occur and who is likely to exploit it. In the Blanchard theft case, the best time to plan to rob the bank was before the money entered the facility. While the actual robbery occurred of course after the money entered the facility, almost everything to make the robbery successful happened before removing the

[99] "eBay - Search: amazon delivery vest." eBay. https://www.ebay.com/sch/i.html?_from=R40&_trk-sid=p2380057.m570.l1311&_nkw=amazon+delivery+vest&_sacat=0 (Accessed Wednesday December 28, 2022).

money. Prevailing security best practices did not account for identifying nor disrupting intelligence gathering. Renowned diplomatic security expert and author Fred Burton explains that much of diplomatic security focuses on bad actors' disruption of surveillance and intelligence activities. This is when nefarious characters are the most vulnerable. If you can spot these activities, you can prevent or disrupt the attack before it occurs. The same is true for protecting supply chains. We have to understand when our supply chains are being surveilled.

Once a bad actor gathers crucial information about a vulnerability, they can apply it against your enterprise. If that doesn't work, they can try it against your tier 1 supplier. If that doesn't work, they can try it against your tier 2 supplier and on down the supply chain. If you go deep enough, you will find a vulnerability, whether physical or digital. This is the crucial flaw of focusing on risk during the supplier onboarding phase. Risk is likely introduced long after the contract is signed. Armed with this knowledge, we need to take a harder look at shoring up both physical and digital security.

A quick search on YouTube will show some very concerning results about all aspects of corporate physical security. The Modern Rogue channel has a video in which they partnered with Red Team Alliance security group to illustrate how to bypass radio frequency identification badge readers. That's right: there's a YouTube video (several in fact) that show just how useless the badge readers are. For a couple hundred dollars and perhaps a construction vest, nearly any corporate ID badge checker can be opened with two screws and a small electronic device dropped in that will capture the code of each badge scanned. It's shocking how easily you can then clone badges. Even worse, the badge access of all employees can be tracked to determine when the building is likely to be empty.[100] Every enterprise that uses electronic ID badges has a massive security vulnerability waiting to be exploited. And even if your company doesn't have this vulnerability, chances are nearly every third party you interact with does. Security guards and video cameras can help, but unless the guards are focused on this instead of dealing with building access, or someone is intently watching the security camera, then physical security remains a huge risk.

[100] The Modern Rogue. "How to Bypass RFID Badge Readers." YouTube video, 16:44. January 29, 2020. https://www.youtube.com/watch?v=Ccm1caB6bao&t=774s (Accessed May 11, 2023).

When is risk?

Nearly all third-party risk is concentrated at the onboarding phase. The bank robbery example perfectly explains the problem of looking at risk at the wrong time. When working with third parties, we need to stay on top of what the entity is doing and how we are working with them. And we need to be attentive to offboarding as well. With the bank robbery example, the security was lax before the cash arrived; however, the opposite is true when it comes to third parties. We tend to focus on onboarding and give minimal to no interaction at the offboarding phase. This is where not knowing the exact number of suppliers you are transacting with matters, and why you need to remove all suppliers that you are not actively managing and tracking. For active suppliers you need to be monitoring what activity they are conducting in your systems and interpreting it for untowardly behavior. This supplier intelligence can help you identify bad activity before it becomes a crisis. Keep in mind that your supplier may not know that it has been compromised so it is incumbent on you as the host system to be on top of anomalous behavior by your suppliers and third parties.

I had a very senior government client proudly state that nearly all their risk mitigation efforts occurred at the supplier onboarding phase. But once the supplier is part of procurement, no one gives them a second thought. This person was from a government entity responsible for physical systems that employ significant digital components. As a taxpayer, this is infuriating, but as a global citizen, it's even more concerning because these systems are used globally, and malfunctioning can create crises. So clearly understanding the third-party activity and the individual components is paramount. Also, who is monitoring all the components that went into these systems? And who is monitoring the third party and its subsidiaries to ensure they are still secure?

Intelligence: risk visualization is basic

Every enterprise has a bevy of risk illumination/visualization/signaling that functions as their left-of-boom activities. And most enterprises have a list of all the potential threat vectors, showing what has happened or is happening. However, it's important to remember that none of this is risk intelligence or risk management. Risk visualization takes all kinds of data input and visualizes it. With a few exceptions, it does not analyze it (what could happen) nor create intelligence (what we should do). For example, risk visualization tells us there is a ship stuck in the Suez Canal and what products are on it. Risk management is how we respond to the situation, and risk intelligence helps us prevent it from happening again—or, ideally, it informs us not to enter the canal in the first place.[101] Intelligence is created with deep interrogation of previous disruptions. The event gave rise to a plethora of news stories, pundits, and analyst declarations about the *Ever Given* ship being stuck, but how many people lost interest in it after it was dislodged from the sand bank? Do we appreciate the significant dependence global shipping places on harbor pilots? What happens when harbor pilots are overworked, undertrained, or simply don't get along with one another? A closer look at what happened on that fateful day should send shudders through the global logistics industry. The subsequent trial revealed some serious and concerning operational weaknesses.

Another problem with risk visualization is that the information is delayed because it takes time to collect and process the underlying data. Thus, risk visualization is not real time, so by the time threat information makes its way to the business, it's not telling anybody anything they didn't already know. Risk tool software providers frequently reference a hurricane approaching to demonstrate the power of their tool—as if the tool detects the hurricane and will tell everyone about the impact. However, anybody who lives in the path of a hurricane already knows that a hurricane is coming and takes the necessary precautions, so the risk visualization tool does not really add any value. To put a finer point on this, imagine an earthquake hitting the San Francisco Bay Area. We don't need a tool to tell us an earthquake hit the region, but we do need to know how our third parties are affected. The problem is that the crisis will be well underway—if not resolved—before the tool can get the relevant information and by then it is too late to be of use. (See Figure 15: *Typical risk threat vectors* on page 123.)

---

[101] After the *Ever Given* was freed, Bloomberg reporter Kit Chellel went to Egypt to report on the aftermath and court hearings regarding the ship. What he learned should be concerning to every supply chain manager/architect/leader. Not only is the canal hard to navigate, but ships traversing the canal also rely on harbor pilots provided by the Suez Canal Authority. According to the testimony, the harbor pilots directing the *Ever Given* that fateful day disagreed and, according to witness accounts, gave conflicting orders to the ship's crew. This illustrates some concerning questions about how global supply chains can be disrupted by individual actors and third-party agencies.
Chellel, Kit. "The Inside Story of the Ship That Broke Global Trade, Bloomberg Quicktake: Originals." Bloomberg Quicktake, June 24, 2021. https://www.bloomberg.com/news/features/2021-06-24/how-the-billion-dollar-ever-given-cargo-ship-got-stuck-in-the-suez-canal (Accessed May 11, 2023).

Figure 15
Typical risk threat vectors

Operational

Ability to supply
- OTIF/ lead time
- Supplier continuity plan ...

Quality
- Quality issues
- Counterfeit ...

Compliance

Government regulations
- Commercial violations
- Safety violations ...

Organizational policy
- Contract violations
- Code of conduct ...

Financial

Financial health
- Financial ratios/ solvency
- Bankruptcy history ...

Pricing
- Labor costs
- Commodity price volatility ...

Ownership
- M&A activity
- Sanctions ...

Macro-economic
- Currency volatility
- Market sentiment ...

Cybersecurity

Breach
- Internal network attack
- Data exfiltration ...

Cyber robustness
- Firm cyber assessment
- Email security ...

Geographic

Geopolitical
- Sanctions and embargoes
- Tariffs ...

Socioeconomic
- Access to skilled labor
- Unemploy- ment levels ...

Infrastructure disruption
- Government funding
- Transportation robustness ...

IP rights
- IP protection/ enforcement ...

ESG

Human rights
- Unfair labor practices
- Labor injuries and fatalities ...

Patient/ consumer safety
- Patient mistreat- ment claims
- Product recalls ...

Animal safety
- Animal mistreat- ment claims ...

Social justice
- Claims of injustice at supplier
- Impact on community ...

Environmental damage
- Carbon footprint ...

DEI
- Gender equality
- Minority ownership ...

Reputation
- Consumer sentiment
- Negative persona ...

Health outbreak
- Develop- ment and maturity of healthcare system ...

Sustainability
- Government treaties and agree- ments ...

Source: Kearney
Notes: OTIF is on time in full. DEI is diversity, equity, and inclusion.

Enterprise risk visualization tools are one of the most enigmatic genres of solution ever developed. They look immensely cool. The leading providers all have some combination of a map plotting risk areas, a list of threat types, and fancy charts denoting red/yellow/green status, all of which is usually set against a black background to maximize the wow factor. The more advanced solutions have pretty network maps (which no mortal has ever figured out how to interpret) and usually a mobile interface. This begs the question: How could something so pretty be so useless?

The trouble with risk is that the most significant threats come from the places where the data is hardest to find. As supply chains have become globalized, the closer you get to the source material and the early production phases, the less transparency there is. This can be the result of failed/failing/repressive governments, local oligarchies, bribery, fraud, language and literacy barriers, proximity to the supplier, or simply a lack of infrastructure. Risk is often introduced very deep in the supply chain long before there is data to track. So here's the question: Are you analyzing the data you have and ignoring the data you need?

The last major issue with risk visualization platforms is information overload or the Chicken Little phenomenon. It's great that you can sign up for risk alerts, but how many alerts do you need to receive in a day before you realize that 99 percent of them are useless? This is usually followed by turning off the alerts. The reverse problem can be true as well, where the threat signal comes through after the event because the data processing takes so long. So, the crucial question is: Is anybody taking any notice when there's a real threat?

People: humans are most of the problem

In cyber right now, it's all too easy to overwhelm systems (people and technology) with low-cost threats and overload the systems into breaking. Consider every employee in your organization. Everything they do introduces a threat to your IT system. However, you'll have (let's hope) an IT organization that puts significant effort into securing your corporate network, which is good and was very relevant when most of your work was done at the office. Now that you work predominantly from home, you're introducing greater risk. Look around your house: How many devices are there? Each person has at least a laptop/desktop computer and a smartphone. Then look at the number of IoT devices, baby monitors, security cameras, home control (Alexa, Google), Internet-enabled toys, and televisions. And you likely have at least one router serving all those devices. How secure are those devices? Are they up to date on all their patches? How secure are the passwords? Do you know what the password is to your router? Did you know there are scenarios in which your router will reset the password back to "password," assuming you changed it in the first place? Can a hacker drive by your house, crack your router, attack your IoT devices, and plant malware? A hacker can monitor your work laptop, waiting for an unpatched vulnerability. When they find it they will use your computer to attempt to phish credentials from your co-workers because the messages are coming from a "trusted source." But now you are a compromised "trusted source," and you don't know it. So now I can social-engineer my way up the food chain. If you don't believe me, just check out how easily one of the largest social media platforms was taken over (and tech companies are supposed to be good at cybersecurity).

The Twitter takeover

In July 2020, Twitter was taken down by a few clever phone calls and some smart social engineering. Teenagers Mason Sheppard, Nima Fazeli, and Graham Ivan Clark managed to bypass all of Twitter's security and take control of dozens of high-profile accounts—including those belonging to Barack Obama, Bill Gates, and Joe Biden—and send fake messages soliciting money through a Bitcoin scam.[102] All too often digitally native companies are held up as the standard bearers for security and aspirational operations. And yet these vaunted Twitter employees readily (and presumably accidentally) gave over usernames and passwords to their internal systems—just another reminder of how poorly governed these companies are when it comes to basic controls. Turns out that all that "speed to market," "disruption," and general thumbing of noses to the status quo is still susceptible to human fallibility. Unsurprisingly, these hackers simply called their targets and spear phished them using false identities until they got access to an internal user administration tool.[103] There

[102] Barrett, Brian. "The Twitter Hack Could Have Been Much Worse—and Maybe Was." Wired, https://www.wired.com/story/twitter-hack-could-have-been-much-worse/ (Accessed November 8, 2022).
[103] Tidy, Joe. "Twitter hack: Staff tricked by phone spear-phishing scam." BBC News. https://www.bbc.com/news/technology-53607374 (Accessed November 8, 2022).
Greenberg, Andy. "The Attack That Broke Twitter Is Hitting Dozens of Companies."Wired, https://www.wired.com/story/phone-spear-phishing-twitter-crime-wave/ (Accessed November 8, 2022).

were so many security breakdowns in this example, but ultimately it came down to the hackers gathering intelligence about the people they called, including come brand-new employees, in addition to knowing about the existence of the administration tool. Basic acting skills convinced the employees to turn over the requisite information.

Wired senior writer Andy Greenberg described how easily an attack like this can happen. "They ask them [the target] to navigate to a fake login page address … and enter their credentials. Another member of the hacking group immediately obtains those details and enters them into the real login page. The real login page then prompts the victim to enter their two-factor authentication code. When the user is fooled into typing that code into the fake site, it's also relayed to the second hacker, who enters it into the real login page, allowing them to fully take over the account."[104] That is the explanation of how this happened. Taking a more holistic view, this hack happened because security designers put a disproportionate amount of trust and responsibility on the weakest part: the humans.

Tools: why I don't get excited about off-the-shelf risk solutions

There are many ways to approach employing a risk management solution. Typically, companies build a bespoke solution in-house, or buy single-domain solutions, and/or a risk platform. The internally developed bespoke solution makes use of in-house or external consulting software and analytics resources and often includes some sort of web scraping, direct data feed integration, and internal data collection. This data is fed into an internal database, processed, and then visualized through some sort of tool such as Tableau or Power BI. The process can be operationally slow and limited to publicly available data (many useful data sets require costly licenses). The analyses also lack the power of the network effect (the network effect pools assets— in this case, data—across companies and creates synergies that benefit all participants that make use of the network). The resources engaged are rarely experts in suppliers, supply chains, or risk. This approach also commonly lacks anything beyond a dashboard-type capability.

[104] Greenberg, Andy. "The Attack That Broke Twitter Is Hitting Dozens of Companies." Wired, https://www.wired.com/story/phone-spear-phishing-twitter-crime-wave/ (Accessed November 8, 2022).

The other option is to buy off-the-shelf, domain-specific risk providers. These solutions focus on a particular information domain and do it especially well. Some examples include financial risk, cyber risk, event risk, reputational risk, and so on. These providers supply deep coverage and analysis in their domain as they tend to acquire data directly from the source. These tools simply represent visualization of the data intelligence value chain. This is not bad, but it is neither risk intelligence nor management.

The next level of evolution is the risk platform. Risk platforms acquire data directly from multiple individual data provider sources. This gives them broader coverage than domain-specific tools. The risk platforms often pay for and integrate key data subscriptions and split that fee across all clients, making it more cost effective. They will also offer the option to integrate domain-specific risk providers to expand the level of coverage. This gives them a comprehensive set of risk signals. Armed with this array of data, the platforms can generate various risk scores and the associated charts and maps. For many enterprises this is hugely beneficial and even for the largest enterprises this can be a great intermediary step.

But despite the seemingly comprehensive view provided by a risk platform, there are limitations. These platforms don't cover industry-specific needs (for example, food safety, conflict minerals, commodity provenance). The risk scoring and modeling is a black box and usually not easily extensible or customizable. The functionality to manage and respond to risk is perfunctory (almost an afterthought), lacking the comprehensive robustness required to manage a crisis. Most importantly, integrating internal data sets can be a challenge not only because it requires sending valuable intellectual property outside the four walls, but also because of the unique nature of internal data sets. Ironically, this can be an unacceptable risk when it comes to customized formulations, recipes, and other such trade secrets.

The biggest issue I have is that these tools do not enable risk analytics or creation of risk intelligence. It is the latter that's crucially important. Take any macro disruption: the way it affects a telecoms company will be far different than a CPG company even though their target consumer is the same. This is because the raw materials, manufacturing, and logistic networks are totally different and have vastly different constraints (cost, supply, capacity, and so on). The intelligence that will help the telecoms company avoid risk will be different than that for the CPG company. This is the nature of risk; the intelligence needs to be specific and unique, and it is hard, if not impossible, for a platform provider to economically produce this level of sophistication across industries or even for companies within the same industry.

Corporate risk theater

Corporations in the main (I acknowledge I am making a very broad generalization here) engage in their own production of risk theater. The senior chief information security officer of Ava Labs, J.M. Porup, identifies five examples of this:

— **Bad security awareness training.** Porup argues it is a waste of time and makes people dismissive of legitimate security concerns.

— **Complex passwords no one can remember.** People keep using variations on the same password with different special characters or, worse, post it on a sticky note (admittedly I have done this more than once).

— **Third-party questionnaires.** These are good for establishing legal liability but do nothing to make the organization more secure. Porup describes the forms as an exercise for third parties to demonstrate how much lying they can get away with.

— **Checkbox compliance.** You take action or buy software or a device because some best practice or governance group told you to. Again, this provides legal liability but does nothing to protect against risk. As Porup extolls his readers (emphasis added), *"Compliance is not securityyyyyyyy ... Compliance is not securityyyyyyyy ... Compliance is not securityyyyyyyy."*

— **Overreliance on antivirus software.** We are in a post-antivirus era. Experts across the board point out that antivirus tools were more useful for a period when software providers like Microsoft spent more time ignoring security threats instead of fixing them. Now, with better architected and auto-patching operating systems, the opportunity for viruses to do wide-scale exploitation is not nearly as fruitful to hackers.[105] Using antivirus software is okay, but companies should not rely on it as a protection mechanism. Why not? The answer is simple—the weakness in digital systems is the humans who run them. These days it's far easier to trick users into downloading an infected file or to respond to a phishing attempt—neither of which antivirus protects against.[106]

These pretty much sum up most enterprise risk theater, at least as applied to third parties. Porup says that "you cannot break security if you do not understand a system better than the people who made the system, and you cannot defend your organization if you do not understand how those systems work to the same degree."

Is your risk management a performance too?

If you have more than 1,000 suppliers, take a bow—you're performing risk theater. No enterprise has enough resources to cope with more than this number. For argument's sake, let's say you have 30,000 suppliers; you are not managing 30,000 suppliers. It would be nearly impossible to manage this many external entities. Or, to put it in a different way, if you have 30,000 suppliers, you are not securing your supply chain vulnerabilities. This translates into extreme exposure risk for your operations. Whether it is fraud, cyber vulnerabilities, or simply accidents, putting so many unmanaged entities into operational systems should send a shudder through every CISO.

Instead, you should consider moving 29,000 suppliers out of your systems into a solution that specializes in the management of third parties at scale. By doing this, you are creating a layered defense of your systems. Think of this solution as a tool you can use to increase security without overreliance on people. However, you should still retain and collect the data from the third-party provider to incorporate it into your supply chain control tower and various intelligence modules.

[105] Migdon, Brooke. "Why experts say you don't need antivirus." The Hill, December 1, 2021. https://thehill.com/changing-america/enrichment/arts-culture/583831-why-experts-say-you-dont-need-antivirus-software/#:~:text=Antivirus%20software%20is%20mostly%20useless,is%20another%20obstacle%20for%20hackers (Accessed May 11, 2023).
[106] Axionadmin. "Why Your Antivirus is Useless Against the #1 Security Threat to Your Business." JUERNTech, December 23rd, 2019. https://www.juerntech.com/2019/12/23/why-your-antivirus-is-useless-against-the-1-security-threat-to-your-business/ (Accessed May 11, 2023).

Once you move the many third parties out of the system, you can start to manage the remaining 1,000 suppliers. First, you must break down the 1,000 into two logical segments—the top 100 and the remaining 900 (approximately). This allows you to use risk tools more effectively, and from there you can build bespoke intelligence.

People play an important role here because, like the Secret Service, they are the last line of defense. Therefore you must train your people to think like hackers and create a culture of distrust (note I said distrust—not rudeness; there's a huge difference). Most enterprises are built to be positive and trusting. They trust that what the supplier represents in the RFP response is accurate. They trust the self-attestation of the supplier on risk and ESG surveys. And they trust that suppliers are who and what they state they are and that employees review invoices properly and compare them against contracted terms and performance.

Sadly, when it comes to people, there's reason to be concerned. Humans are fallible, so it's not surprising when companies like Volkswagen fake smog tests or individuals falsify quality tests for steel used in submarine hulls for the US Navy.[107] These are the decisions and actions of imperfect humans. Trust is good, but we must verify that no risk actually exists, that we aren't overpaying, or that our suppliers aren't polluting on our behalf. The fact that enterprises don't have more disruptions can be attributed mostly to luck—because the majority aren't verifying to the necessary level. If people are your first and last line of defense, you might simply be playing a part in corporate risk theater.

The Miyagi-Do approach to risk

Fans of Netflix's *Cobra Kai* series were treated to an important risk management concept in season five, episode seven, entitled "Bad Eggs." In this show, 12 students of the Miyagi-Do dojo are each asked to take an egg and protect it. The students take their eggs and scatter across the grounds in an attempt to keep each of their eggs safe. Their sensei Chozen Toguchi goes one by one and smashes all the eggs in a series of increasingly entertaining ways. The

---

[107] Johnson, Jean. "Metallurgist Admits to Faking Steel Test Results." Yahoo News, November 8, 2021. https://www.yahoo.com/news/metallurgist-admits-faking-steel-test-231848638.html. (Accessed May 11, 2023).

students failed the lesson and are forced to do it again. The second time around, the students figure out that if they put all their eggs in a single basket and surround it, they can provide 360 degrees of protection. This time, as their sensei attacks, they can move, shift, and protect as a collective group, making them successful.

In a highly disruptive and volatile world where the threats are ever increasing, each enterprise attempting to protect itself alone will end up with its own broken egg. Case in point: let's say that Enterprise 1, Enterprise 2, and Enterprise 3 all use the same supplier, Sunrise IT. Each enterprise asks Sunrise IT to fill out a security questionnaire. Of course, because Enterprises 1, 2, and 3 are all special flowers, they have different wording and questions on their form. Now Sunrise IT has to put resources into filling out all three surveys. Assuming Sunrise IT fills each out accurately (a dubious proposition), all three enterprises have to evaluate the responses (and that assumes they actually do that). Who from each enterprise is evaluating the survey response? What are they learning individually about Sunrise IT from the response? It would be far more effective for all three enterprises to use a single questionnaire, ideally collaboratively provided. This streamlines the process for Sunrise IT. Because there is less repetitive busy work, it's more likely that it will provide comprehensive answers.

Working with Sunrise IT collaboratively also creates a far more robust outcome in terms of data collected and understanding it. It allows for back-and-forth clarifications, learning, and greater sharing of information. Now imagine if there were 10, 20, or 30 enterprises. Think about it as a reverse supplier day, where instead of one enterprise inviting many suppliers to collaborate, you bring many enterprises together to work on the collective risk with a single supplier—in this case, Sunrise IT. Of course, you can't do this with 30,000 suppliers—only with your top 100. And there would undoubtedly be a vast number of legal and competitive hurdles to overcome. But the takeaway is that we need to work together across enterprises to do a better job at stream-lining the task of the suppliers and enhancing the collective risk posture. Otherwise, we are all vulnerable. Make no mistake: no enterprise has enough money and technical resources to combat nation-states. However, greater learning and sharing of information among the collective will vastly improve the collective security posture.

The risk strategy we really need

As companies' risk management capabilities mature, there will come a time when they need to move away from a fixed strategy to a perpetual hacking approach. This gives us more flexibility to respond to known vulnerabilities while creating space to explore and identify unknown attacks. For example, one could identify that one of the biggest known threats to production is a demand shock, as we saw during the pandemic with toilet paper, sanitizing wipes, and PPE. By comparison, a category manager who is responsible for cocoa plantations in Sierra Leone probably knows what's happening on the individual farms they contract with. But do they know what's happening in the local/regional/national governments? Do they understand the logistics networks serving the farms, or even simply the surrounding infrastructure (roads, bridges, ports, and so on)? It is this kind of risk extrapolation that will come to define tomorrow's risk management strategies.

Quixotically, risk management is crucial to running an enterprise. But left unchecked, one can spend so much time and money on risk management that the very act becomes self-destructive. Thus, the right questions to ask are: Should we treat all risks equally, or should we prioritize some over others (say, cyber over financial)? Once we've identified and prioritized the relevant risks, we need to map what internal and external data we have, what data we need, and what data we don't know how to get. This will answer the question of whether we're analyzing the data we have or the data we need.

Additionally, when we apply the hacking mindset, we aim to collect as much data on the third parties in our supply chain. Then we turn that data into intelligence (see Figure 7: *The data value chain* on page 31). There are three keys to success. First, collecting data is easy, but you need to be able to rapidly cull through the data to determine what is relevant and accurate and what isn't. This is where analytics tools can really help (as described in Chapter III, *Intelligence: data underpins everything*). The second is to understand the actual risk. It is unrealistic to address every threat vector against every supplier. By prioritizing impact on the business, we can focus on managing the risk that is most likely to impede operations, whether it is a $10 capacitor from a fourth-tier supplier or obtaining sufficient PPE, both of which can shut down a manufacturing line. By contrast, the biggest risk to a financial institution might be data exfiltration or vulnerability to ransomware through their systems integrator. Third, and perhaps most importantly, you must work to simplify the number of third parties. As you can see, the hacking approach is not a traditional strategy that gets created and executed, but rather a change to the company's DNA.

How I would infiltrate your supply chain

Every supply chain is under attack these days. Many of these attacks fail, and others go unreported. Then there are the high-profile ones that splash into news feeds such as the recent attack on SpaceX. A ransomware gang claims to have hacked Maximum Industries, a tier 1 supplier that fabricates rocket parts for the space company. The hackers threatened to post many of SpaceX's component drawings and internal operational documents for the world to see.[108]

To drive home just how vulnerable every supply chain is, I want to illustrate how straightforward it is. If I want to hack your supply chain, I would gather intelligence, figure out the best tools, and employ the necessary human capital. To start I would decide whether I want to disrupt your operations, steal your specifications, redirect payments, or take control of your machines to wait for a future opportunity. For argument's sake, let's say I want to take control of your laptop so that I can read your email, documents, and capture your passwords. One way to accomplish this is to spear phish you. However, I would have a higher probability of success by creating a fake company, say a contract manufacturer. I could use Chat GPT to generate a fake website offering a high-demand service such as 3D printing. I would then create a fake LinkedIn profile, use a click farm to create thousands of connections, and create a fake executive team with pictures of people who do not exist (persondoesnotexist.com). Then I could develop a few spec sheets with all our capabilities and post them on the fake website. As an added measure of legitimacy, I would register on the supplier networks and buy Google ad words so that when people search for a supplier to work with multiwall polycarbonate, acetal sheet rod tubes, and plexiglass, I pop up. I could even go a step further

---

[108] Montgomery, Blake. "Ransomware Gang Claims It Hacked SpaceX Supplier, Threatens to Leak 'Certified' Designs." Gizmodo, March 15, 2023. https://gizmodo.com/spacex-lockbit-ransomware-gang-leak-designs-threat-1850228968.

and purport to be a diverse supplier. The end game is getting you to download the spec sheets from my site.

Once you do, that would execute the ransomware. Your virus protection doesn't stand a chance. If I wanted to siphon off payments, I could simply buy a defunct business that had Fortune 500 companies as clients. The defunct company would likely be an approved supplier and in the enterprise payment system. What if I just started submitting invoices for work done? What are the odds that at least a portion of them would get paid? This is why we have to stop and reflect on where and when attacks can happen.

Hacking risk management: five takeaways

— Good risk management improves your individual security and builds resilience.

— Ask yourself when risk is likely to occur.

— Don't forget about physical security.

— Good acting is one of the biggest risks.

— You can't manage more than 1,000 suppliers, otherwise you are performing risk theater.

Chapter IX
Protecting future supply chains from the boom

"Even with all our technology and the inventions that make modern life so much easier than it once was, it takes just one big natural disaster to wipe all that away and remind us that, here on Earth, we're still at the mercy of nature."

– Neil deGrasse Tyson, American astrophysicist, author, and science celebrity

Risk is everywhere and nowhere all at once—whether it's crossing the street, driving to the store, using a cellphone, or base jumping off skyscrapers. We're continually learning about risk, from childhood and finding out about the world to when we're old and in need of care from others. We pass these risks on to our kids, our friends, and others with whom we come into contact. Watch out for the rattlesnake over there or don't get involved with that pyramid scheme. When it comes to protecting our supply chains, we possess the skills necessary to at least identify the likely vectors of attack, so how do we make risk identification and mitigation an everyone opportunity?

Risk is liminal, not in your fancy boxes

Risk does not fit nicely into boxes that match organizational employee hierarchies. Risk has no boundaries; it lives in liminal spaces. Liminal spaces occupy the space between two existing things. For example, the time between dusk to dawn, which is neither night nor day, is a liminal space. As we design and secure supply chains we need to look for the liminal spaces between our organization and our third parties. That is where today's risk lives. It's also where tomorrow's risk lives. The thawing of the Arctic, the exploration and colonization of Mars, and ownership of cyberspace are just a few examples of risks sitting in liminal spaces. For example, who owns cyberspace? Is it the Internet backbone providers? Is it the cloud infrastructure providers? Is it the nonprofit organizations? Is it governments? We live in the digital age where we rely so much on instantaneous communication, so we had better get a handle on this.

Again, this highlights the limitation of risk visualization tools: they show that which is known—useful for situational awareness—but they do not show us the liminal risk, that which is unknown.

Hacking makes our supply chains stronger

In 2013, my brother had an illuminating experience when he stepped into a hotel elevator with his then seven-year-old daughter, Kalea. Upon entering the elevator and without prompting, she started punching buttons on the elevator in a seemingly random sequence. When asked what she was doing, Kalea responded by saying that if she touched the elevator buttons in a certain sequence, the elevator bypassed all other floors and went straight to the lobby. My brother, a CISO and certified security specialist, was blown away. He asked her where she learned that trick, and she said a video on YouTube. It never occurred to my brother, or even myself, that we could simply search for a hack to bypass stopping at other floors on the elevator.

Hacker, cybersecurity specialist, and associate professor at Emory University Ymir Vigfusson delivered a TEDx Talk entitled, *You Should Learn How to Hack.*[109] Vigfusson's argument is that "everyone should know how to hack because you can't play effective defense unless you understand the offense." If we as a community have any chance of securing our global supply chains, we need to start thinking about how nefarious characters are looking to break our operations. He highlights three traits of hackers: failure, curiosity, and experimentation. The whole process of hacking is predicated on failure, much

---

[109] Vigfusson, Ymir. "You should learn how to hack." TED, April 2021, https://www.ted.com/talks/ymir_vigfusson_you_should_learn_how_to_hack (Accessed May 11, 2023).

like the variability associated with gambling. Hackers may spend days, weeks, or even months failing at their objective, but as Vigfusson notes, "failure is something that hackers are particularly good at; in fact, failure just energizes us to keep going, to keep hacking, to try to push the boundary of the system that we're trying to tinker with, and it just increases the bliss that we feel once we ultimately break in."

Perhaps the most important skill hackers possess is curiosity. They always look at a target and consider where the vulnerabilities reside. Systems, whether analog or digital, are designed to operate one way, and hackers look for ways to make the system work in other ways that suit their needs. In the analog world, imagine you live in a bay area city and on a one-way street that has a history of devastating fires. Over time new people move into the neighborhood, and because they don't know the history, they engage in dangerous and illegal behavior, such as parking in such a way that impedes emergency vehicle access or using open fire pits. Let's say you notify the city, but they don't have a process or willingness to notify the neighbors. Can you hack the system to change neighbors' behavior? What if—hypothetically speaking—you create a mailer with the City of Oakland and the Oakland Fire Department logos, and you clearly articulate the local fire history and city ordinances, all information presented in a way that conveys authority? If you did such a thing and the neighbors started changing their behavior by parking legally and not blocking the road, then this would be an example of hacking an analog system (again, all hypothetical of course).

For cyberhacking, it's similar but even more precise. Digital systems are constrained by the embedded software. For example, login pages require an underlying action after the user submits their username and password. But if you figure out what the underlying system is expecting, in this case a properly formatted username and password, then you can modify the input you provide. For example, when you enter the username and password you can include some extra code that gets executed. The underlying system cannot defend against the extra code submitted because it looks only for a username and password. Once we can successfully talk to the underlying system through the login page, then we can start asking the system to take actions like showing all the users in the database. In his TED Talk, Vigfusson illustrates this for the audience.

Take these two examples and apply them to a supply chain with 30,000 third parties and you can start to see the exponential problem of analog and digital hacking. How many of your processes can get socially reengineered? How many of your digital systems can be manipulated if nefarious characters flood them with unexpected data? I believe that each of us in our respective organizations should look at how third parties can be used to introduce risk. When third parties know the enterprises better than the employees working for them, that is a problem. We often see this with software and tech providers, but it is also an issue with consulting and legal providers. The relationships developed with the business, and especially leaders, can leave the enterprise vulnerable to misinformation attacks (deliberate or accidental), cyberbreaches, and physical threats.

Vigfusson says that failure, curiosity, and experimentation are the building blocks of hacking culture. Deployed against our organizations, the approach is terrifying—but used internally, this culture of hacking will make our enterprises more secure.

Creating our own culture of hacking will lead to better cyberpractices and help overcome the fraud that is cybersecurity education.

The biggest risk to your supply chain operations is email

You and I will get hacked in our lifetimes (if you haven't already on LinkedIn, Hotmail, Yahoo, and elsewhere). This was unfathomable just a decade ago but, given the preponderance of information we store digitally and the increase in successful cyberattacks, you should expect all your data emails to be dumped online. You should expect that you have malware on your phone or your PC at any given time. And you should most assuredly expect to be hit by ransomware. We are at war. Let me rephrase that: every country is at digital war with every country. All countries are continually spying on one another. One crucial way we can protect ourselves from these threats is to stop sending important information via email.

We need to think like a hacker and try to understand how a nefarious character would attempt to breach our supply chain systems. Not every enterprise uses SAP; not every enterprise uses Oracle; not every enterprise uses AWS. But every enterprise uses email. And email is a very insecure protocol. Therefore if I am a hacker, I am going to target the most widely used insecure tool: email. This begs the question: Why are we sending emails with links and attachments, whether they're RFPs, specifications, or even invoices?

I have a CPG client that accepts about 90 percent of supplier invoices through email. This makes it super-easy for the suppliers; they simply generate an invoice from their finance system and email it. Once the email is received, the payables clerks manually enter the information into the finance system for payment. If there are questions, the clerks go back and forth with the supplier over email to clarify and fix errors. To put this in perspective, most of my clients have at least 70 percent of invoices through an e-invoicing system. I thought this couldn't get any worse until I explained the problem to the client, who was not grasping the seriousness of the problem, so I went to their public webpage and found the email address for where to send invoices and a very helpful list of fields to fill out when submitting an invoice. I'm sure this information was put on the website to reduce the number of emails back and forth between suppliers and my client's finance department. While that makes sense from an efficiency point of view, in terms of security this is a disaster waiting to happen. If I take a hacking mindset to this, I could simply generate a random and fake invoice and send it in. Naturally (and hopefully) the AP clerk would figure out that my invoice was fake. But how much effort was expended doing that? What if I submit 100, 1,000, or 10,000 emails per hour? Resources have to be expended to address each email. However, it gets worse. By design, if I'm sending an email with an invoice attachment, the AP clerk has to open the email attachment. What if my fake invoice is really ransomware waiting for an unsuspecting person to open it? Remember the first rule of all the useless cybertraining: don't click on the attachment. So why has my client put human users in a situation where they have to open the attachment? The way to solve this is to plumb the supplier's finance system to the [pharma client's] finance system or move the supplier into a third-party solution that puts in layers of defense. This is where digital fluency comes into play. Middle managers (including my client) need to be aware of these security gaps. Accepting an invoice solution that is not directly connected to suppliers is a dereliction of duty and a major breach waiting to happen.

The fact that we're not using collaboration tools for third-party management is setting us up for digital breaches. We need to stop emailing documents. We will know we have succeeded when we use fit for purpose collaboration systems to share information directly, sourcing tools for bidding events, SRM tools for relationship management, and P2P systems for invoicing. Of course, this means we need a smart front door to organize this for suppliers.

Data exchange with third parties will come to define the 21st century supply chain. Whether it is risk management, ESG opportunities, innovation opportunities, supply assurance, legislative compliance, or simply creating an efficiently running supply chain, everything will increasingly rely on a steady stream of data. That means we will need to plumb a continual data flow from supplier systems to our enterprise systems and back again. But data exchange is not enough; we have to take that data and make it meaningful by understanding how the business objectives can be changed, modified, or enhanced by what's happening in the world. For example, let's take an oil and gas company that wants to get into electric charging stations. First, there's procuring the charging technology. That is simple enough and will come from a new set of suppliers. Of course, the near monopolistic demand power that O&G companies held in the age of carbon no longer applies here. The underlying components of EV chargers rely on downstream electronic components that feed many other technology devices such as smartphones, tablets, and automobiles. Additionally, many entities, such as local/state/federal governments, are putting in EV charging stations. Then there is the question of real estate; do you put EV chargers at existing gas stations or do you create EV-only stations? And since consumers will need to wait while their car is charging, does this change where you locate these stations and the types of services provided? Perhaps most importantly, because EV chargers can be smart devices, they can call back to the corporations that own them. Again this is an example of the reverse flow of data back into the supply chain system.

So here we have a clear example of collecting data and payments that get transferred directly. This presents a few problems and opportunities. For example, we need to be able to collect the payments and process them. Then we need to ensure that they are being maintained, which can be optimized significantly better by collecting and analyzing the data coming back. And then of course we need to make sure that we are doing proper risk management. Because if you install an EV charger, as a nefarious actor, all I have to do is buy (or steal) one of the said chargers, tear it down, hack it, and learn how to bypass all the controls so that I can route the payments to my bank account. Speaking of banks, drawing back to the robbing a bank example, how many EV chargers are left unattended for days, weeks, or months on end before they are operational? How closely are they being monitored? Look at any new parking lot construction, and you will see EV charging spots and technology being deployed long before the lot becomes operational. The Idaho National Laboratory did an extensive teardown on electric vehicle charging equipment and found the underlying operating system was running an old, non-secured version of the Linux operating system. These holes compromise the systems, making stealing both financial and personal information possible. Or these systems can be taken over and used as zombie machines to conduct distributed denial of service attacks. Hacking electric vehicle charging stations is not a "what if" philosophical musing; shortly after the Russian invasion of Ukraine, hackers compromised charging stations near Moscow as a show of solidarity for Ukrainians.[110] So the question for every supply chain that deploys and supports smart devices and infrastructure and relies on third-party providers is: What are you doing to ensure the equipment is free from and protected against bad actors? This is not something that a survey or a news scraping tool will surface.

Designing supply chains for simplicity

In a globalized, disruptive, and digital world, understanding your enterprise systems in relation to third parties is the most important activity. For every third party in your systems, you must know who they are, why they are there, and when they are leaving. Correspondingly, when it is time for them to go, you must politely but successfully escort them out of the physical and digital systems. How many suppliers, contractors, and third parties have some physical access to your enterprise? More importantly we must build a defense in-depth (DID) posture in relation to our third parties. That means building concentric circles of defense around our systems. Most enterprises have

[110] Interestingly, I wrote this as a what-if philosophical musing after watching new charging stations be installed on the campus of Nevada State University and be left unattended for months. Then I came across this article that brought home the reality of this threat.
Lemos, Robert. "EV Charging Infrastructure: Electric Cyberattack Opportunity." Dark Reading, March 3, 2023. https://www.darkreading.com/ics-ot/ev-charging-infrastructure-electric-cyberattack-opportunity.

some sort of supplier segmentation to identify suppliers in cascading levels of importance, based on what they supply and the amount of money spent with them. Typically, this is meant to categorize suppliers by value.

Basic DID theory suggests that we should have an intermediary solution that is the first point of interaction with our systems. Then as suppliers move to a greater volume, value (amount transacted), and strategic importance they can graduate into the core enterprise systems. Otherwise they should sit in a third-party system and the relevant metadata (who was paid, when, how much, and core supplier information) should be shared. This creates a level of separation between the third party and the enterprise systems.

When it comes to attacking your supply chain, nefarious third parties don't care about your organizational structure, your governance, or roles and responsibilities. Enterprise organizational matrices and technical silos prevent the free exchange of data within the company. While this might be good for confidentiality, IT management, or middle management job preservation, this is a killer for risk management. In fact, the more silos the better because less internal sharing of information makes the enterprise less secure. Take, for instance, a healthcare client with separate supply chain and procurement organizations. The procurement organization is tasked with third-party risk management. The supply chain organization is tasked with risk to products and materials. Further, a risk center of excellence (CoE) sits somewhere between the two. The supply chain risk owner looks at material and product risk, while procurement looks at risk from the supplier. On paper, these organizations are supposed to share information. But after talking to them for about two minutes, it's clear they are more concerned with who owns what rather than how to protect the enterprise. This leads them to develop competing tools and capabilities, but without the entirety of the risk data set. If we're doing third-party risk, we must understand the products and materials impacted by each supplier. Conversely, you can't understand the risk to a product or a material if you don't know everything about a supplier, namely all of the suppliers' locations, operational capabilities, cyber/physical/financial posture, and the n-tier suppliers. Therefore, if we are even going to increase the risk management maturity, we need to do our part to create free-form sharing of information.

The zero trust concept

One of the most important security methodologies to come about in the past decade is the concept of zero trust. Zero trust, originally conceptualized in a white paper written by Google, assumes that your systems will be breached. It frames the security mindset not to trust any user's device by default, no matter where they originate from, until the device can be properly authenticated. Additionally, there can be zero trust segmentation that further groups and isolates particular devices and users. An oft-cited example is ransomware on a single computer that can be quickly isolated before it spreads to other devices.

Further, zero trust calls for the continual monitoring and mitigating impact of a breach. It's important to note that zero trust is a concept that must be adapted, expanded, and customized to every organization. It is meant to be an organizing principle: a singular approach to clarify roles, expectations, and ways of operating internally and externally with third parties. Zero trust is best done with education and collaboration among third parties. It is not a dictate, but rather a method to create a secure way of operating.[111] The advantage of a zero trust approach is that it generates the necessary visibility and auditability to effectively respond to and learn from breaches.

Naturally, our next-generation supply chains need to be built on a zero trust methodology. Unfortunately, we have been going in the wrong direction on this. Given the embedded IoT devices, AI, and robots (physical and virtual) and the preponderance of third-party entities, there is far too much unmanaged information flying around. The failure of big ERP has led to an explosion of point solution supply chain tools, and a get business done at all costs mentality has eviscerated most attempts at a logical security apparatus. In other words, our current third party security design is broken. To build the next-generation supply chain, we need to implement a zero trust design. Experts estimate that half of all malicious attacks affect small and medium-sized businesses. That means that large numbers of your suppliers are under

[111] Keary, Tim. "A practical approach to building resilience with zero trust." VentureBeat, August 13, 2022. https://venturebeat.com/security/a-practical-approach-to-building-resilience-with-zero-trust/ (Accessed May 11, 2023).

attack and likely compromised at any given time, whether they (or you) know it. So now is the perfect time to address these problems.

What does zero trust for a supply chain look like?

The answer to this will be unique for every enterprise. Please do not read what follows as a treatise or manifesto for the definitive zero trust approach. Rather, this is meant to start a discussion about designing and building zero trust into our supply chains. We need to debate, challenge, and expand what it means to build zero trust supply chains. Using the Mitre ATT&CK framework, which is an open source knowledge base of cyberattack techniques and tactics, I created a guide to the components necessary to secure supply chains.[112] This is meant to start the discussion, not be the authoritative perspective.

Zero trust: intelligence

— **Enumeration.** Understand the components of your supply chains, the third parties, and what adversaries might do.

— **Threat vectors.** Understand who your adversaries are and what they might do. Identify the characteristics of an attack.

— **Situational awareness.** Know what's happening in your systems and what are the anomalies.

— **Adversary emulation.** We need to hack our systems. We need to attack each individual component to see if the protections are working as expected. We must test reactions to an unexpected event.

— **Shadow systems and devices.** Let's stop pretending that everyone is using the corporate-issued laptop that is locked down. This checks the box for the CIO, but absolutely kills productivity. As a result, users will find workarounds that are even worse. For example, our Kearney laptops are locked down

[112] MITRE Corporation. "Getting Started with ATT&CK." MITRE, October 2019. https://www.mitre.org/sites/default/files/2021-11/getting-started-with-attack-october-2019.pdf (Accessed May 11, 2023). Axiomadmin. "Why Your Antivirus is Useless Against the #1 Security Threat to Your Business." JUERNTech. https://www.juerntech.com/2019/12/23/why-your-antivirus-is-useless-against-the-1-security-threat-to-your-business/ (Accessed May 11, 2023).

in such a way that you can't add a home printer because of "security concerns." A former colleague bypassed this by simply emailing documents (insecurely of course) to their personal email account on their personal machine and printing from there.

Zero trust: tools

— **Ring-fencing.** This means each third party accessing your systems needs to be contained from wreaking havoc on your systems, users, and other third parties. Ring-fence each system so that the compromising of one system doesn't take the whole thing down.

— **Multifactor authentication (MFA).** Access control is usually managed by something you know (like a password), something you have (key fob, token), or something you are (biometric). Multifactor authentication means you have two or three of these. MFA needs to be applied to any connected smart device. We must also apply MFA to improved API security.

— **Applied security methodology.** Many IoT and digital devices are easy to compromise because they either lack security, have not been patched, or still use default security credentials. More importantly, consider who is managing said devices to ensure they remain fully patched.

— **Unmanaged, unsupported tools.** Sometimes the greatest security comes from reducing the number of systems, like those 15 supplier portals or SharePoint sites that were spun up for no good reason.

— **Dark data.** This is data that sits unused within an individual computer, a cloud account, or across the organization. It is literally and figuratively a toxic asset. Because we don't see the data, we forget it exists. It is all the files we collect but haven't opened in years. It is the multiple versions of documents, the tools we signed up to try but never bought a license for.

— **Individual enhancement.** The most common way to attack your supply
chain is through phishing or social engineering. We need to train people not
to click on the link. We must teach them to phish so they can understand
the patterns of phishing and social engineering versus the rote memorization
of yesterday's attack.

— **Don't punish failure.** If people click on the link and ransomware their
computers, we must not punish them. We need to take the opportunity
to teach our users what happened so everyone can learn from it. This will
allow us to build greater awareness and increase our collective ability to
fend off these attacks.

Today we can apply zero trust proactively and voluntarily. But as governments
continue to apply more scrutiny and oversight, it will become more common-
place. Moreover, anybody seeking cyber insurance these days will find out that
insurers are requiring significantly more and comprehensive protections before
underwriting policies. Simultaneously, they are increasing the number of
exclusions. This means that the insurance industry is taking cybersecurity vastly
more seriously than in the past.[113] (See sidebar: *You can think like a hacker* on
page 147.)

Secure supply chain design: digital twins and multi-enterprise visibility

The digital twin, a digital representation of a physical object, is one of those
great phrases that has cachet and gravitas and can be used for product
design, manufacturing, and functional operation of a product. For example,
you might have a hydroelectric dam. One could create a digital copy of the
physical asset and feed the copy operational data so that when you look
at the digital version, it's akin to looking at the physical dam and its operations.
This is a very powerful tool for supply chains. Too often, we struggle to get
basic visibility (that is not Excel based or real time) into our end-to-end supply
chains. However, it is ever more crucial to have this capability as part

---

[113] Chen, Elena. "Cyber Insurance Underwriting Changes." Woodruff Sawyer. April 30, 2020. https://
woodruffsawyer.com/cyber-liability/cyber-insurance-underwriting-changes/ (Accessed May 11, 2023).

You can think like a hacker

Visualizing the risk across a global supply chain can seem overwhelming, but most of the work involves asking the right questions. Here's an exercise to get your mind used to asking risk questions:

You and I are standing outside your house or your apartment. What does the physical security look like?

— Are the doors locked?

— Do they have deadbolts?

— How many spare keys do you have?

— Who has them?

— Are your windows locked?

— Do you have an alarm?

— Do you have a dog or two?

Let that go

— Now same exercise, but from a digital point of view. We're standing outside your house.

— How many digital devices do you have?

— How many laptops, tablets, and smartphones?

— How many smart thermostats, cameras, refrigerators, garage door openers, sprinkler controllers, baby monitors, toys (Barbie dollhouses), drones, Apple watches, gaming consoles, and Alexa devices do you have? Are they all patched?

(continued on next page)

You can think like a hacker (continued)

— If you have kids, do you know what apps and websites they're going to and what malware they're bringing back?

Let that go

As we're standing outside your house, what prevents me from accessing those devices on your network? Your router or firewall? Is it patched? Do you know the password? Has the router reset itself and defaulted to the generic password? I can try that or I can just crack your Wi-Fi password because the encryption used is very weak; I'm afraid you have some significant gaps in your digital security. This is just the beginning of this exercise; each of us every day is creating large amounts of digital exhaust (email, e-commerce, text, WhatsApp messages, social media posts) that make us susceptible to cyberattacks.

This visualization aims to help you see where risk lives. Risk management is unlike any other supply chain function: there is no playbook, and you can't prescript it or learn it in an online course. The risk factors, how we operate supply chains, and the business structure are all constantly changing. Imagine the vaccine example we discussed at the beginning and how much opportunity there is to introduce risk into your supply chain.

Nobody is going to walk up to your front door and attack. They will find the vulnerability nobody suspects, exploit it, and then take a free ride up the supply chain. That's what SolarWinds was about. This is why a whole risk classification is called "supply chain attack." It's nefarious actors, and it's equally accidents and mistakes. So I want to ask you: Where are the weaknesses in your supply chain? If you knew all of them, would you have trouble sleeping at night? In more practical terms, everyone who operates any part of a supply chain has the wherewithal to identify and remediate supply chain vulnerabilities. In other words, you already have the knowledge—you just need to know where to look.

(continued on next page)

You can think like a hacker (continued)

Despite the triteness of my last statement, what I am suggesting here is that to do risk management effectively, you need a culture of curiosity. You need to create an environment that supports this open line of inquiry or, more succinctly, you have to start hacking your supply chains. For example, how many of you take the annual "security training" each year? Inevitably there is going to be a "phishing" module, which will try to teach you how to spot a malicious email and what you should do or not do with it. If you click on the link, what happens?

The main takeaway here is to take nothing for granted. Nobody is as secure as they think they are. The moment people say they are secure is the moment they are most vulnerable because they don't understand the magnitude of the problem. More problematically, risk management is not just a singular problem but a collective problem. (See Figure 16: *Elements of a supply chain control tower* on page 150.)

of creating more secure supply chain designs. This is important given the complexity that third parties bring to the equation, especially when it comes to crucial operations like contract manufacturing, contract packing, and 3PL providers. The digital twin helps solve this problem by combining all this third-party data into a singular supply chain control tower for end-to-end visibility. This enables us to apply end-to-end intelligence in service to security, which improves risk management and resilience.

Say we have 10 contract manufacturers, all operating at various levels of capacity. Ideally, we will have a view into the inventory and capacity of all 10; that way, we can allocate orders based on capacity. But what happens when one manufacturer suddenly stops operating due to a disruption? How do we rebalance the capacity with the others? If the OEM owns all the manufacturing facilities, they should have the visibility within their network to rebalance and reallocate. But because all the contractors are external in this example, how do we get the data we need to understand this decision? The same applies to

Figure 16
Elements of a supply chain control tower

— Capability to control, measure, and
quickly respond to supply chain events

— Access to real-time, relevant data
linking physical events of the supply
chain to information and action

— Management structure and process
with clear roles and responsibilities
focusing on continuous improvement

— Agile and scalable technical solution

Source: Kearney

collaboration, where we need to share visibility into forecasting and production and track the back-and-forth changes with our suppliers.

Here the digital twin concept is so useful to secure supply chain design. If we take this example further, we can start to model future outcomes. You can visualize the optimal outcomes and inefficiencies. This is where a dashboard is an old construct. Instead, we can just "ChatGPT it" by asking an AI-powered interface to tell us the answer (I am using ChatGPT only for illustration purposes). This is the level of sophistication we need. Ultimately, greater connectivity to multi-enterprise and effective data exchange allows us to repurpose and rebalance nimbly across third parties.

Near-term decisions, long-term ramifications

Many companies are underutilizing today's solutions and leaving a lot of their capabilities on the table. It's like using a Ferrari to drive the kids to school or dogs to doggie daycare. All too often, we're solving visibility problems from 10 years ago. Many of the supply chain issues we're dealing with today are there because of the choices a previous generation of leaders made. These folks acquiesced to IT. To every supply chain leader out there today, your choices will have effects long after you retire. It's not too alarmist to say that even the existence of the company might have as much to do with what the current supply chain leadership implements. I hate to frame it this way, but it's time for some hard truths.

If yesterday's mistake was fealty to big ERP, today's leadership mistakes are believing in an AI solution. I watch all these AI solutions go in, generate hype, and then splutter as they try to scale. The reason is obvious: the data is not where it needs to be. Therefore, I have little interest in AI solutions. I am extremely focused on solutions that improve data collection and management at scale. These solutions excite me because once I have the data, the algorithms will naturally follow. More importantly, this is where our algorithmic literacy and digital competency come in because, with the data, we can use the power of AI to create bespoke intelligence for our organizations.

Hacking supply chain design: five takeaways

— Risk sits in liminal spaces.

— Make it simple, make it secure.

— Stop using email to run your supply chain.

— Design for zero trust.

— Employ digital twins to model third-party risk.

Chapter X
Building digitally savvy supply chain leadership

"Digital is never done."

– Karoline Dygas, chief procurement officer, Nordstrom

"In war, only the simple succeeds."

– Paul von Hindenburg, president of Germany's Weimar Republic

You can buy or build all the technology you want and mandate all the cyber-security and digital tool trainings in the world, but unless you have digitally savvy leaders, efforts to secure your supply chain and make it more resilient will fall flat. The leadership changes include challenging narratives we have about users and how we embrace boosting adoption of digital tools.

Conversely, most business leaders don't truly understand the power and impact of digital. If they did, they would treat it as the existential threat and growth opportunity that it is. Organizations' traditional ways of working are limited by historical precedent, which on the surface isn't bad. If it's working, keep doing it. However, it becomes problematic when you're trying to change the enterprise and initiate a digital first way of operating. And then there are some people who lack the motivation to evolve.

People don't like change because it adds more work for them in the short term. Oftentimes they either don't understand what an unconstrained future could look like or they simply recognize that the broader organizational culture rejects meaningful change. It's easy to fight change. It's easy to come up with an outlier excuse of why something won't work. Given this organizational inertia, most companies don't consider the full scope of op model changes. The top-down approach usually fails because the goal is to change hearts and minds. For example, nearly every large company has gaggles of data scientists, but where do they sit? In the business, in a center of excellence, or both? How does the enterprise effectively deploy these resources? All too often it's a mishmash of initiatives and suboptimal in practice. In a digital world, where the business is empowered to do what it needs and possesses the proper skills, then this whole discussion will be moot. In other words, we need to bring the business to the data science.

The digital upskilling of people is often distilled down to the minimum effort possible: taking some learning management courses. Digital transformations are often big and complicated, so there are great opportunities for poor performers to hide. Even worse, they can be active blockers to success. Or you will see employees adopt the language du jour to protect themselves (for instance, the person who builds reports is now a "data scientist," which is nonsense).

The scope is a huge issue as well. Often digital transformations are too big to manage and are focused on activity, not productivity. A big digital transformation is counterfactual to a digital way of working. A digital way of working would be agile, whereby activity is managed in a nimble way to increase success and limit risk. So why is the transformation itself a complicated and monolithic waterfall that's almost guaranteed to lead to failure? (I blame executive desires for a big bang and consultants for perpetuating this.) Most digital transformations are too reliant on storytelling and promoting. The "why" is usually well articulated, but the "what" and "how" are always missing (especially the how). Hence the need for a transformation true-up (see *The transformation true-up* in Chapter I, *The vaccine story*).

Disrupting the deficit perspective

I love patterns. There's something so gratifying about studying a particular topic and over time discovering new patterns. Sometimes they are obvious, such as sitting through a steady stream of technology start-up pitches and recognizing the buzzwords everyone is slinging around like a bartender serving happy hour beers. Other patterns emerge slowly and are more pernicious. As

I started traveling again after the pandemic, I noticed significantly more digital competency and maturity than before it. That alone wasn't terribly surprising. However, when I started to hear nearly every analyst/consultant/start-up solution provider talk about how broken procurement was, it gave me pause.

Here's some of what I heard: Procurement …

— *"has no real control over the category, is remote from every purchase, and has no analytics or insights to effect change or improvements."*

— *"has zero ability … to influence sustainability objectives, manage demand or supply chain risk, or deliver basic category management."*

— *"continues to run many activities manually, using traditional technology."*

— *"can't answer business questions timely."*

— *"team collaboration and audit trail are poor."*

— *"has no visibility into spend."*

— *"is backward-looking reporting; there's no forecasting."*

— *"struggles to be influential in business decisions."*

And CPOS …

— *"are often unable to learn from past issues to effectively plan, implement, or execute any lessons learned holistically to prevent future disruptions."*

— *"are unable to devise long-term strategies for dealing with a disruptive world and think beyond procurement to envision products and innovations that can be manufactured despite disruption."*

While many of these statements may be partly true, they are mostly platitudes meant to sell something. They've become shorthand for saying that the procurement organization has problem X and the supplier has solution Y. All we need to do is match the two and the problem will be magically solved.

But they are lies that we keep repeating until that's all we can see in the professional mirror.

Getting supply chain leaders out of the "idiot box"

One of my favorite military historians is Dr. Michael Neiberg, a professor at the US Army War College and author of a number of WWI monographs. He spends a lot of time advocating change in how WWI is taught.[114] One of the mistakes he encourages us to avoid is putting the people of 1914 into what he calls "the idiot box." This is "our instinctive response to see the people of that fateful year as uncommonly stupid or bloodthirsty, provid[ing] us comfort that we are too smart or too sophisticated ever to make the mistakes they made." While the stakes are not nearly the same, it feels like analysts, consultants, solution providers, and the like have put the collective supply chain profession in the "idiot box." As evidenced by the examples above, supply chain professionals are cast as incompetent and unfit to do their jobs. Reading these quotes independently would lead someone to conclude that supply chain professionals simply sit around eating sprinkled donuts and working on their fantasy football teams. But the reality is that many of these criticisms result from supply chain design rather than individual incompetence.

Over the years, I have been critical of supply chain organizations for many of these same themes, especially regarding digital decisions. And surely there are organizations that still struggle with these issues. However, is it fair or even accurate to cast these blanket assertions? Coming off a series of major global disruptions over the past few years, for which supply chain professionals bore the brunt and stepped up to the challenge, it is clear that these statements don't hold up to scrutiny. The real issue with these statements is that they hold the profession back. The profession can't advance if we take such a deficit view. It becomes self-reinforcing fratricide. It's not that everything has to be awesome or perfect. But we have to be able to effectively credit progress and advancement. More to the point, we need to look for positive trends, even if it means we can't sell yesterday's solutions, offerings, or technologies.

---

[114] Typically it is taught as four causes (MAIN: Militarism, Alliances, Imperialism, and Nationalism). His argument is that is too simplistic and provides false comfort: "[i]f we can convince ourselves that those four MAIN factors either no longer exist or are no longer an existential danger to peace, then we can go to sleep at night in the belief that the horrors unleashed in 1914 really do have nothing to teach us." Neiberg, Michael S. "Ukraine and World War I." National WWI Museum and Memorial. April 8, 2022. https://www.theworldwar.org/learn/about-wwi/ukraine-and-wwi (Accessed May 11, 2023).

Principles of digital leadership

The fundamental truth of the digital age is that leaders need to understand how digital tools work. It's not that leaders don't have a million other concerns and responsibilities, but not understanding digital (tools, data, and analytics) can have catastrophic effects. Look at how easily Chelsea Manning and Edward Snowden simply transferred gigabytes of incriminating data without the knowledge of any supervisor or leader. Manning, an army intelligence analyst with access to highly classified information, burned 750,000 files onto DVDs, labeled them as Lady Gaga, Taylor Swift, and other musicians, and walked out of secure intelligence facilities—and right out of Afghanistan—unchallenged.[115] This is a staggering breach considering that military intelligence facilities are supposed to be the most secure.

To effectively manage our third parties digitally we must ask ourselves the following questions:

— **Is it too complicated?** Most technology fails because it is too complicated.[116] Users rarely use hard-to-navigate or hard-to-understand technology. This is especially true for suppliers.

— **Is it adaptable?** We should be making it easy (and self-service) for suppliers to integrate into our systems. And we should offer them help should they need it. If it takes six weeks to integrate a single supplier into our systems, we're doing something extraordinarily wrong.

— **Am I properly incentivizing my third parties to participate?** Is there a benefit to the third party? For example, perhaps you offer better payment terms to suppliers who use the system. If there is a benefit, highlight it. If there's not, just stop the initiative.

---

[115] Manning, Chelsea. *Readme.txt* (New York: Farrar, Straus and Giroux, 2022). The Daily Show. "Chelsea Manning - README.txt." YouTube video, 7:53. October 17, 2022. https://www.youtube.com/watch?v=Ofkd1-P_LI (Accessed May 11, 2023).
[116] DPW 2022. "Bullets, bombs, & blunders: what modern war teaches us about digitizing supply chains." YouTube video. 24:13. October 3, 2022. https://www.youtube.com/watch?v=mPLGfHpv3KA&t=1308s (Accessed May 11, 2023).

Here are some practical principles that should guide digital initiatives. Feel free to incorporate some (or all) of them:

— **Automate, automate, automate.** And if you can't automate it, make it self-service.

— **Start with smaller projects that deliver big value.** While this sounds exceedingly basic, fixing a customer visibility issue, a production downtime issue, or an employee onboarding issue will create ten times the goodwill of any big bang project.

— **It's all about the common core infrastructure.** Build on an advanced stack (like AWS/Azure/GCP) with a strong data foundation. Make use of the libraries provided by the cloud provider to build bespoke solutions and augment those with the relevant point solutions.

— **It's all about multi-enterprise collaboration.** The greatest risks come from your third parties. The greatest ESG opportunities come from your third parties. The most inefficient parts of your supply chain come from your third parties. The solution to all three is to get good at multiparty data interchange.

— **Break artificial organizational constructs.** The biggest enterprise needs (UX, risk, ESG, innovation, and so on) don't fit in silos anymore. For example, think about the customer experience: they want a quick and easy way to purchase, receive, and return their item, all with status updates and provenance information. That objective alone crosses a bunch of different systems (sales, ERP, 3PL, and countless others), but the customer doesn't care.

— **Digital is something you do.** You don't learn digital from a learning management system (LMS). LMS programs are a sign of digital immaturity, the quintessential check-the-box exercise. You need the motivation to learn, experiment, and ask for help. Anyone can learn anything on the Internet if they have the motivation and are willing to put in the time.

— **It all gets back to make versus buy.** In a world with hundreds of thousands of new technology companies, it's important to understand when to buy (and customize) or build internally. Finding the balance here is crucial because it's easy to get pulled in different directions.

— **Fund digital projects like a venture capitalist.** Project funding should be contingent on progress (like VC stages).

— **Adopt a product and platform approach.** Move from project managers (cat herders and timekeepers) to product managers (value orchestrators or CEO of the product). Think product life cycle (design, development, deployment, maintenance, improvements). This includes integration to other systems and leveraging data into and out of the product. Product managers must always center the user; whatever you build should benefit the user.

— **Separate business as usual from innovation.** This must be a hard line, otherwise people will get drawn into the day-to-day firefighting and innovation will slip.

— **The CIO is either in the boat or out of the boat.** If they're in the boat, they must be rowing. If they aren't, then paddle away. The CIO must be an evangelist and a cheerleader.

Watchouts and fixes

— **Broken agile.** Most companies have "corporatized agile," meaning they have bastardized it to use agile language on old ways of working. A sprint is four weeks max. If you're talking about sprints in more than that, then you're doing agile wrong.

— **Intentionality.** Don't throw out random digital solutions; if users can't see how it will land, they won't engage.

— **Stand up a product management function.** It's important to have product managers who understand each solution's short- and long-term success. They must have clear KPIs that measure customer usage and satisfaction.

— **Clearly define success for every function.** What passes for digital supply chain transformation success is embarrassing. Set a clear goal so it's easy to tell if you are achieving it.

— **Blowing things up is easy.** It's the rebuilding that's hard. Avoid wholesale ripping out of digital systems as this creates unnecessary drama. Adopt a model of layering on top of existing solution gaps and phasing out over time.

— **Scaling is a struggle.** Everyone gets stuck in the test-and-learn phase. That's the easy and fun part. The implementation is hard. Leaders have to lead when things get messy. You need to get your hands dirty as solutions roll out.

— **There's no such thing as a "best-in-class process."** Today's systems need to be intelligent. That means you no longer need to hard code decision tree logic into the processes. Instead, entire processes can be replaced by an interactive bot that guides, directs, and influences based on user metadata and input (as ChatGPT is starting to do).

— **It's no longer business as usual.** Business is dynamic and changing. Our suppliers become our competitors. Our competitors become frenemies.

— **Digital complexity is IT's problem.** We need simplicity for the user experience at the expense of IT.

— **Stop the waiting game.** If you're waiting for a tech provider to deliver features in a future release, you'll likely be waiting a very long time.

— **Find, build, and sustain the translators.** A business will succeed based on its ability to balance technological capabilities and business needs, so you need people who can translate and bridge the knowledge gap.

— **If you criticize it, you fix it.** The way to deal with skeptics of process design is to ask them to do the task at hand and see how much they enjoy it.

How leaders infuse digital to the organization

— **Motivate your employees to operate digitally.** Asking employees to cut and paste information is a clear communication that you do not value them. Asking employees to use an archaic web-based tool that was designed in the early 2000s is a clear communication you do not value them. It is your choice to do this, but you can't espouse moving to digital if your actions don't match.

— **Lead by example.** Make sure you use the same tools as your employees because if you are frustrated, they are too. If you pioneer the use of new tools or techniques, then people will follow. Fear of missing out (FOMO) is real in digital adoption.

— **Get your current people comfortable with digital.** There are two sides to this issue. On the one hand, you need to convey that everyone has an opportunity to make the journey (and if they don't, tell them). On the other, if they don't make the changes and progress in their learning, then you have to move on. It's unfair to let people flail in a digital world. These people will impede progress.

— **Hire different profiles.** The entirety of human knowledge is at our fingertips. We have tools that code applications, write essays, and solve mathematical or engineering problems. Therefore your team needs to have a different set of profiles and experiences. This is where diversity is finally going to have its moment because an eclectic mix of profiles will harness the power of digital way better than 1,000 engineers from an engineering school or 1,000 MBAs from a business school.

— **Create open-ended initiatives.** Give people projects that engage the brain, stimulate creativity, and require critical thinking skills. For example, have employees build systems (physical and digital) then attack them, reimagine the constraints to designs, or simply challenge the business-as-usual status quo.

Hacking supply chain leadership: five takeaways

— Leaders need to be digitally savvy.

— Stop putting supply chain leaders in the idiot box.

— Ask yourself hard questions about your approach to digital.

— Everyone makes the same mistakes; learn from them.

— Lead by example: infuse digital principles top down.

Chapter XI
Hacking ESG

"Question to supplier: Do you measure your green-house gases?

Supplier answer: We don't have any; we're not in the agriculture business."[117]

Globalization fundamentally reshaped business for the first two decades of the 21st century. One of the enduring side effects of this change was the digital connectivity that came with the "flattening" of the global business environment. As global supply chains grew, shipping raw materials to China for manufacturing, packaging, and shipping to regional distribution centers and individual stores required vastly more connectivity and data exchange. Cloud computing, new fiber networks, smartphones, 5G, commercial space operations, new sensors, and computing devices have further shrunk the world by bringing more data to countries, companies, and even individuals. While all of us are still improving said collection and analysis of all this data (as explored in Chapter III, *Intelligence: data underpins everything*), there's an unexpected benefit to putting this infrastructure in place. Greater connectivity, data collection, and computing capacity empower us to take a bigger stake in creating the world we want to see.

The analyzing and sharing of all this information make us more informed consumers. It also allows us to take a more proactive role in addressing the

---

[117] This quote has been modified for readability and anonymity, but the sentiment remains the same. Thank you to Alex Gershenson for providing it.

issues facing our world, whether it's war, famine, clean water access, human rights, Black Lives Matter, protecting the bees, saving the coral reefs, stopping gun violence, education, microplastics, banning land mines, or any of the thousands of other ills that plague our global society. For example, I don't have to go to Indonesia or Malaysia to see the deforestation caused by palm oil production. I can see it in satellite photos and measure and track its deleterious effects over time without leaving my desk. I don't have to rely on annual reports or reporters to travel there and publish stories; I can literally see it. In the not-so-distant future I expect to be able to dial up satellite imagery on demand, or there will be satellites trained on these hot spots 24/7. This is a staggering breakthrough in terms of information transparency. I fully expect that as the range of sensors and data collection mechanisms expands, we'll continue to have access to vast amounts of new and useful data. This data will fundamentally change consumer expectations, governmental regulations, and regulatory compliance. Moreover, the social media aspect of this will amplify progress on all these fronts. As an example, a news article about Morgan Freeman converting his 124-acre ranch into a bee sanctuary has been catching fire on social media and creating awareness for the declining bee population.[118] The increasing attention to ESG means that companies need to get a whole lot more sophisticated in their efforts. Simply rating suppliers for the annual report is no longer good enough.

I admit that it's easy to criticize enterprises for misguided ESG efforts. I'm not trying to score an easy shot here but rather to start a deeper dialogue on how companies can create more meaningful and impactful ESG initiatives. Before we do that, though, we need to acknowledge that corporations are being asked to do the following (and probably even more). (See Figure 17: *The ESG morass* on page 165.)

This is an ambitious and overwhelming agenda, much like the never-ending list of risk threats. Corporations seem to be asked to take on tasks that governments and NGOs are unable or unwilling to tackle. How can a single company solve systematic racism? I think it may be a little unfair to dump all of this on

[118] Nace, Trevor. "Morgan Freeman Converted His 124-Acre Ranch Into a Giant Honeybee Sanctuary to Save the Bees." Forbes, March 20, 2019. https://www.forbes.com/sites/trevornace/2019/03/20/morgan-freeman-converted-his-124-acre-ranch-into-a-giant-honeybee-sanctuary-to-save-the-bees/?sh=51919231d-fa5 (Accessed May 11, 2023).

Figure 17
The ESG morass

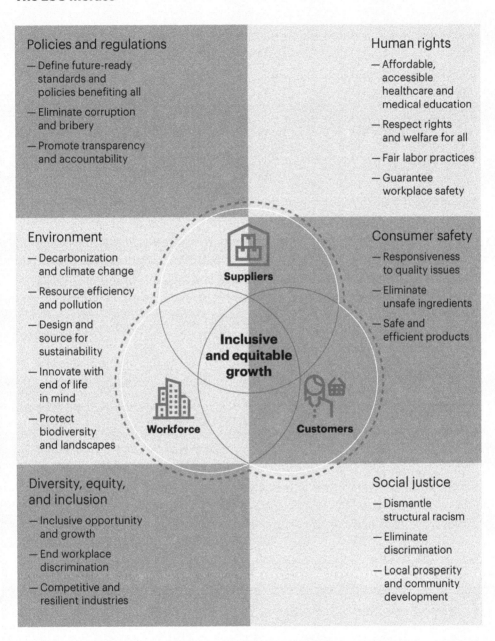

Policies and regulations
— Define future-ready standards and policies benefiting all
— Eliminate corruption and bribery
— Promote transparency and accountability

Human rights
— Affordable, accessible healthcare and medical education
— Respect rights and welfare for all
— Fair labor practices
— Guarantee workplace safety

Environment
— Decarbonization and climate change
— Resource efficiency and pollution
— Design and source for sustainability
— Innovate with end of life in mind
— Protect biodiversity and landscapes

Suppliers

Inclusive and equitable growth

Workforce

Customers

Consumer safety
— Responsiveness to quality issues
— Eliminate unsafe ingredients
— Safe and efficient products

Diversity, equity, and inclusion
— Inclusive opportunity and growth
— End workplace discrimination
— Competitive and resilient industries

Social justice
— Dismantle structural racism
— Eliminate discrimination
— Local prosperity and community development

Source: Kearney
Note: ESG is environmental, social, and governance.

corporations. Most enterprises exist to make money, but that's not to say that companies get a pass on ESG. I would be very happy to see companies stop polluting our waterways or setting rivers on fire,[119] spewing tons of carbon, and hiring suppliers that violate human rights. But, like risk management, we need to focus on what's logical and practical versus doing what governments have failed to do.

In that context, supply chain security and risk intersect with corporate ESG efforts. Both are headed for a reckoning; not a doom and gloom reckoning, but rather a positive and interesting one. While most ESG efforts are laudable, they lack the real-world practicality to truly move the needle on risk management. Most large enterprises use very slick language to show various ways they seek to address supply chain sustainability. That's usually something to the effect of improving manufacturing to reduce, recycle, or reclaim waste, employ recyclable or compostable packaging, reduce scope 3 carbon emissions, and assess suppliers. Many companies are even adding ESG to the board of directors' objectives. These actions and platitudes all look nice on paper—however, in an era where the climate crisis is growing and consumers have access to equally powerful data as supply chain managers, the bar must be set significantly higher. Instead of simply reporting, companies will need to take bolder steps to support the reserving, restoring, and rewilding of the earth's resources.[120]

ESG intelligence: recycling

In early 2021, I was outside my house for an impromptu COVID concert (two guys playing guitars) on our street. I was talking to my neighbor JD Ambati, who's a serial entrepreneur and founder of EverestLabs. As we listened to 1970s and 1980s rock covers, he started telling me about his latest project: to improve the efficacy of recycling centers with robots. I had to restrain myself from visibly rolling my eyes. I was thinking, "You've got to be kidding me with this—another do-gooder trying to ride the ESG hype train." However, when he asked me, "Don't you work with CPOs and heads of supply chains for

[119] History.com Staff. "EPA, Earth Day, Cleveland Cuyahoga River Fire, Clean Water Act." History.com, February 17, 2023, https://www.history.com/news/epa-earth-day-cleveland-cuyahoga-river-fire-clean-water-act (Accessed May 28, 2023).
[120] Simon JD Schillebeeckx & Ryan K Merrill published a 2021 manifesto titled "Regeneration First."

CPG companies?" I suddenly became much more attentive. I told him I did, and I wanted to understand his angle.

JD explained that he was setting up robotic arms on recycling lines to increase the efficiency and effectiveness of recycling in waste management. Using humans to sort trash from recycling is self-defeating and severely limited. A waste line with humans can pick only between one and 15 items per minute, whereas a robot can pick 40–60 items in the same amount of time 24/7 without breaks.[121] Not only can the robots more efficiently remove recyclable materials from the waste lines, but they also observe, catalog, and report on *all* the material that traverses the waste lines. To make the robots work, EverestLabs had to set up 3D cameras to collect and map the data of what was going down each line. From there, EverestLabs engineers wrote proprietary machine learning algorithms to identify each type of valuable packaging in the shortest amount of time (we're talking milliseconds level), then direct the robotic arm to pick these objects and deposit them in the correct bins with the highest success rate. It took the EverestLabs team more than three years just to get their software and robotic end-of-arm tools right. All of that was intellectually interesting but not compelling.

Then he hit me with what felt like the proverbial right hook. The project created a massive source of real-time data about the contents of every recycling line. The AI could differentiate the type of material (aluminum, plastic, paper) and, most importantly, the branding (Coke, Pepsi, Budweiser cans). It took 30 seconds for the shock to wear off. This development had huge implications for ESG efforts because now we can tie sales data with recycling data. Using this data, we can quantify the number of products that are being recycled versus going to landfill. When it comes to environmental producer responsibility (EPR), this allows each brand to determine what proportion of responsibility is theirs. More importantly, it allows us to see landfills as a new source of supply. This means that counting the reclamation (or non-reclamation) of recyclable materials will improve vastly, which in turn will provide a huge opportunity (or a huge problem) for enterprises. Essentially, companies will be hit with a tsunami of recycling and reclamation data. What will that data show?

---

[121] Estimates provided by EverestLabs data scientists.

This all becomes vastly more compelling when we consider that demands for virgin aluminum have been steadily increasing and, in some cases, it isn't even available. The robots in recycling centers can recycle more aluminum from waste lines and increase recycling efficiency. We can get a real-world accounting of our EPR.

In 2018, the total recycling rate of aluminum containers and packaging, which includes beverage containers, food containers, foil, and other aluminum packaging, was 35 percent. Within this number, the most recycled category of aluminum was beer and soft drinks cans, at 50 percent (0.67 million tons). In 2018, landfills received approximately 2.7 million tons of aluminum.[122] While efforts are in place to recycle aluminum, it is not enough. In the US alone, nearly $800 million worth of aluminum cans are lost to landfill. The gap between postindustrial and postconsumer recycling efforts must be closed. The collection process does not need to be the same everywhere but should be more easily understood.[123]

In security and risk management, the question is whether we're visualizing the data we have or the data we need. Often the greatest risks come from the places with the least amount of data (say a government-owned factory in China). If we employ the same approach to ESG, we find that the greatest opportunities are where we have the least visibility. Nowhere is that clearer than in the waste management project JD explained to me. It will show what vast opportunities exist, and it will also show how slapping a recycling logo on aluminum cans means absolutely nothing in practical terms if most of the recyclable aluminum ends up in landfill. Collecting data from hard-to-reach places reinforces the idea that companies need to come out of their ivory towers and look at what's happening all the way down at the bottom of their value chain. More specifically, we can now trace every bit of aluminum going into landfill, which will give governments more actionable data to enforce EPR legislations. So, any CPG using aluminum (especially any that deal with third

[122] "Aluminum: Material-Specific Data." Facts and Figures about Materials, Waste and Recycling. United States Environmental Protection Agency.
https://www.epa.gov/facts-and-figures-about-materials-waste-and-recycling/aluminum-material-specific-data (Accessed July 19, 2023).
[123] Smith, Tricia. "The value of aluminum recycling," Recycling Today.
https://www.recyclingtoday.com/news/workshop-addresses-aluminum-packaging-and-dross-recycling/ (Accessed July 19, 2023).

parties) should take a much closer look at this ecosystem. More broadly, tech companies should take note because this technology and intelligence will eventually make its way into the electronics recycling value chain as well.

ESG tools: beyond scanning, scraping, and surveys

Using data and insights provided by ProcureTech, I spent a good chunk of the summer of 2022 evaluating more than 230 ESG tools (I was putting off writing this book). I hadn't realized there were so many ESG tools. Of that vast number, only five were remotely interesting to me. Subsequently I found an additional seven interesting tools. Everything else is underwhelming at best.

Some of the solutions I analyzed were not relevant (health and safety, consulting, or nonprofits), but most fell into five broad categories: reporting, questionnaire, traceability (human input), offsets, or ratings. All these are laudable initiatives, but they're rather simplistic and problematic. Carbon offsets have been debunked or at least sufficiently challenged to suggest that this is not a legitimate way of solving the ESG problem. ESG questionnaires are as foolish for ESG as they are for risk management (see Chapter VIII: *Risk management: the bridge between security and resilience*). The quote at the top of this chapter is an apt example of this fallacy. Even if suppliers are willing to provide the necessary information, we have to check to see whether they truly understand what's being asked of them (and that greenhouse gases have nothing to do with growing agriculture). Traceability that relies on human input is neither reliable nor efficient. And digital device traceability can be problematic (see the Tony Soprano issue in Chapter IV, *Tools: we are in a post-ERP world; we just haven't accepted it yet*). Despite scraping millions of public websites for information, rating companies are only surfacing and evaluating a highly biased subset of information. Finally, charging suppliers to be audited by a third party once a year suffers from a twofold problem. First, an annual audit allows a lot of risk and environmental damage to be done in the intervening 364 days. Second, how thorough is an annual compliance check? Who's doing this audit and how well versed are they in the topic they're tasked with evaluating, or are they simply asking perfunctory questions to check the box? This begs the question of whether the annual third-party audit is simply ESG theater.

The true impact and ESG opportunity will come from the places that are hardest to see, cloaked behind the secrecy of governments and in otherwise opaque locations. Finally, reporting is great, but building a "carbon cube" or other ESG dashboard is only at the visualization part of the data value chain, restricted to telling you what happened or what is happening. Much like spend cubes, they simply show where the money was spent (which is good) but it doesn't change the fact that whatever amount was spent is no longer in the corporate bank account. Spend reporting can merely be used to inform future negotiations and allocations of work. The same is true for carbon cubes: every ounce of carbon tracked is merely showing what has been expended into the air already, and you can't get it back unless there's some massive carbon capture technological innovation. In short, most of these ESG solutions involve some measure of scanning, scraping, surveys, and reporting, none of which does much to directly change outcomes.

ESG people: palm oil producers and consumers

Palm oil, used in more than half of all packaged products in the US, is under threat amid a perfect storm of skyrocketing demand and unsustainable production processes. We do not need another article denouncing the deleterious effects of palm oil. It is widely known that palm oil production is bad— very bad. The issue became a key theme during season two of the popular Netflix series *Grace and Frankie* when Frankie, played by Lily Tomlin, takes an ethical stand against the corporate use of palm oil. Even beyond popular culture, one can hardly escape the constant drumbeat of negative news enumerating how rainforests are being cleared and burned to produce palm oil, threatening the extinction of orangutans, pygmy elephants, and Sumatran rhinos. This activity alone produces vast amounts of carbon greenhouse gases. Palm oil production is also responsible for human rights violations as small landowners and indigenous people are driven from their land to make way for plantations. And investigators, including 14-year-old Olivia Chaffin, a girl scout in rural Tennessee, have put a spotlight on palm oil producers who use physical and sexual violence and forced child labor.[124]

---

[124] McDowell, Robin and Mason, Margie. "Girl Scout cookies tied to child labor in palm oil industry." Associated Press. https://www.tampabay.com/news/nation-world/2020/12/29/girl-scout-cookies-tied-to-child-labor-in-palm-oil-industry/ (Accessed November 8, 2022).

Any one of these reasons would be enough to eliminate palm oil from our global supply chains, yet one extraordinarily good reason supersedes all the others. The production of palm oil is creating an environmental disaster that will threaten the entire supply of palm oil. For perhaps the first time in history, producing a commodity directly threatens the long-term supply and viability of the commodity itself. We refer to this as a circular risk. Over the past 50 years, demand for palm oil has risen sharply, with annual production quadrupling between 1995 and 2015, and is expected to quadruple yet again by 2050. This ever-growing demand for palm oil and its unsustainable production processes are now fueling its own destruction.

The impending boom

A close look at the supply chain reveals that 84 percent of the world's palm oil is produced by two countries (see Figure 18: *Palm oil production by country* on page 172). In 2020, Indonesia produced 43.5 million tons and Malaysia produced 19.9 million tons. Both countries are starting to face serious consequences of climate change, specifically severe weather events such as heavy rains, severe flooding, and landslides, along with rising sea levels of between 2.4 and 3.8 millimeters per year in the region. In Indonesia, palm oil plantations are concentrated in two islands: Borneo and Sumatra. In 2019, the five leading provinces (Riau, Central Kalimantan, North Sumatra, West Kalimantan, and South Sumatra) produced about two-thirds of all the palm oil in Indonesia. In the past two years, each of these provinces has reported devastating flooding and landslides, repeatedly wiping out communities and killing people. Research suggests these instances occur more often in palm oil villages. Additionally, rising sea levels are engulfing new land masses in these provinces every day.

The situation in Malaysia is nearly identical. A 2020 scientific paper found a negative relationship between annual average temperatures and palm oil production: if temperatures rise between 1°C and 4°C, palm oil production could decrease by 10 to 41 percent because of a decline in palm seeds. Additionally, since palm oil farms thrive closer to the coastline, the rise in sea levels will steadily eliminate the amount of arable land. Taken together, these two trends signal a major disruption ahead.

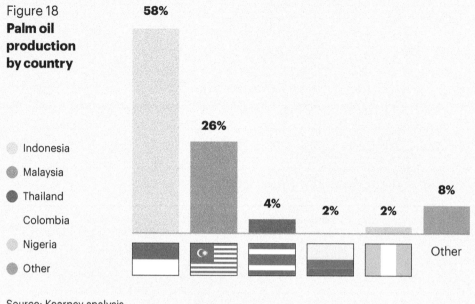

Figure 18
**Palm oil
production
by country**

- Indonesia
- Malaysia
- Thailand
- Colombia
- Nigeria
- Other

58%   26%   4%   2%   2%   8%

Other

Source: Kearney analysis

We're left of boom

The use of palm oil is rapidly shifting from something that has bad optics for individual companies to something that is a high risk, with the long-term supply (and costs) under threat. With their ever-increasing demands for palm oil, companies and consumers are killing their own source.

We can clearly see the boom coming. There's a short horizon between today's status quo and tomorrow's supply shortages and price increases. Companies can make bolder moves now—not just committing to using sustainable palm oil but also switching to alternatives or doing something different. It's better to absorb the switching costs now because prices will skyrocket as the supply is compromised. This is crucial to ensure that the demand for palm oil is kept in check and doesn't continue to accelerate toward total supply destruction. If ever there was a time to redesign, reformulate, and reinvent, it's now.

Applying the hacking mindset

If I had the answer to the palm oil problem, I would quit my great job at Kearney and dedicate myself to the elimination of palm oil like the good liberal I aspire to be. But perhaps we're looking at the problem backward. We assume that the shelf stability of palm oil is the dependent variable here, and finding an odorless, clear, and tasteless oil that will hold up for an equal amount of time is what we need an answer for. However, what if we took a hacker's mindset to the problem? Could we use highly optimized and flexible supply chains to reduce the time from when a product is manufactured to when it's consumed? In other words, can we drastically reduce manufacture–to–consumption from months and years to weeks or days? If we could do this by using tighter forecasting, manufacturing, and distribution, then we wouldn't need to account for such long shelf lives. This would then open up different types of, and hopefully less deleterious, replacements to palm oil.

Hacking ESG: five takeaways

— Addressing ESG is a key part of a supply chain security and risk management.

— Audits, web scraping, and surveys make little tangible impact.

— Look for new sources of meaningful ESG data.

— Build bespoke ESG-based intelligence.

— Approach ESG problems anew with the hacking mindset.

Chapter XII
Is the brave new world real?

"Digital is a game changer."

**– Ninian Wilson, global supply chain director and CEO,
Vodafone Procurement Company**

As a historian I know that the future never plays out in the way we imagine, predict, or hope. So the question I always seek to answer in my research is whether what I'm talking about is real or fantasy. In other words, am I illuminating a path to a destination that's anchored in what we're capable of? Is this future supply chain built around third-party connectivity, efficiency, and excellence possible? The short answer is yes. Though the example is becoming a cliché, Amazon is proof that this future vision is possible. Amazon over the years has built an amazingly robust, expansive, and data-driven company. In fact, as a logistics company they're unparalleled in their ability to use data to influence third parties in support of delighting their customers. What they have done to fundamentally redesign fulfillment centers, transportation, computing infrastructure, technological development, workforce optimization, robotics, ESG, and a litany of other business operations is nothing short of exceptional. It may take a few decades to truly appreciate the genius behind Amazon's redefining of supply chain operations (which does not release them from any harm they have created). From a supply chain point of view, most legacy companies would be lucky to achieve a fraction of what Amazon has. In short, they built tomorrow's supply chain yesterday and have wielded it like Thor's hammer (or Stormbreaker for MCU fans). There are plenty of books, case studies, interviews, and blog postings extolling the virtues of Amazon (and plenty of detractors as well). And I expect thousands more to be produced over the next 10 years. But for this study I wanted to step out of the hype cycle that everyone quickly ascribes to Amazon and look beyond the easy answer.

The question I ponder every night before I go to sleep is, can a 100-year-old company build a next-generation supply chain and, if so, what would it look like? Can a legacy company actually get out of its own way? Can the employees and ways of working step beyond performance reviews, security audits, process redesign, executive approvals, legal compliance, document reviews, objectives and key results, annual planning, H1 and H2 planning, all hands, regional summits, reorgs, and corporate politics?[125] Nearly all my clients spend most of their days in meetings, "communicating" and "collaborating" with one another. I often wonder when anybody has time to do any work. Of course, this is probably why consultants get hired.

Vodafone Procurement Company

As I was conceptualizing this book, Vodafone Procurement Company (VPC) reached out and asked me to comment on an initiative they were undertaking. They had scanned the market for a set of solutions to build their next-generation supply chain and came away unenthused about the market. They decided they would go ahead and build their own tool, so they wanted an independent sanity check. This is usually a good idea if you're going to bet your career on an idea that will cost your organization millions of dollars. We spent almost 90 minutes on the phone, and I was blown away by their scope and ambition. Afterward I told them that I would like to follow up in six months. As it turned out, our next meeting brought me to their corporate headquarters in Luxembourg. This meeting convinced me beyond all doubt that I needed to feature VPC in this book and led to a second trip four months later.

Walking into the VPC offices, you'll notice two very tangible markers of a digital way of operating. First, the design of the offices is very inviting, egalitarian, and exudes modernity. Living in the shadow of Silicon Valley, I have seen a lot of start-up spaces, and the VPC offices feel like they could be in downtown San Francisco or Santa Clara—minus Lego bricks in the conference rooms and

---

[125] Seshadri, Praveen. "The Maze is in the Mouse." Medium, February 13, 2023. https://medium.com/@pravse/the-maze-is-in-the-mouse-980c57cfd61a. (Accessed May 11, 2023).

free meals. What struck me was that CEO Ninian Wilson and his team had built a culture of digital anchored by a strength in intelligence, tools, and people. They operate more as a 21st century digitally native company than the legacy company they formed out of.

Intelligence

Located on level three of the offices sits the most functional architectural centerpiece I've ever seen in a corporate setting: a colossal six-panel touchscreen measuring 140cm by 420cm (55in by 165in), the focus of the entire floor. Think of it as six panels, each 2ft by 4ft, all touch screens. It's like a gigantic iPad. The screens display the key metrics (compliance, savings, health and safety, claims, payment days, shopping experience) necessary to run the business. Each chart, graph, or other indicator can be double tapped to see the underlying data. Ninian Wilson conducts his key meetings around this board, giving him and his team the necessary situational awareness. It's important to note that it took them a long time to obtain all the data they needed to get this working properly. Even in the time between my trips, I noticed some key additions. (See Figure 19: *Vodafone Procurement Company touchscreen* on page 178.)

There is complete agreement on the data that feeds all their operations and business planning. That is a staggering statement, considering that when Wilson took charge individual teams hoarded data in silos (a situation most enterprises struggle with). He describes how it took many weeks to collect data in Excel and by the time it was ready to show the business, it was out of date. Naturally the business summarily dismissed it.

By contrast, these days if there's a question about data provenance or why something is showing as an outlier, they track it down and explain it on the spot. There's a collective mindset around using key performance indicators to improve the quality of data. This has a direct benefit on operational activities and management. There is no hiding behind bad data or middle management obfuscation. Each person I talked to showed a strong comfort with data, how to get it, and how to use it. As an example of how deep this capability goes, category management is the foundation of VPC's operations. The company is in the process of moving to intelligence-based sourcing and category management. To achieve this aspiration, category managers are

Figure 19
Vodafone Procurement Company touchscreen

Source: Vodafone Procurement Company

not only required to submit their strategies but also to submit data plans that detail desired ways in which new data sources and enhancements could improve performance.

The VPC team has been able to democratize data across the organization. The elusive data democratization and effective usage of said data is perhaps the most significant difference between the big tech companies (Netflix, Amazon, Apple, Google) and traditional enterprises. Putting in a centralized analytics platform and visualizing the data (on the fancy display wall) changed the company's familiarity and attitude around both the data itself and the visualization of it. For proof of this change, Wilson looks at the analytics platform access logs to note that each day there's a spike between 8:45 a.m. and 9:00 a.m. from a supply chain point of view to the system as people are starting their days.

Wilson is quick to point out that they're not doing enough in the realm of predictive insights and intelligence creation. However, they're among the most sophisticated procurement and supply chain organizations in terms of creating and operating in a culture of data. Moreover, they're embarking on an ambitious agenda: they're rolling out an innovative new program where they're taking their ERP data and moving to their underlying cloud infrastructure so they can mix it and match it with other data sources. This includes a program to get good at exchanging data with third parties to generate an advantage. As an example, VPC is procuring solar energy (as of this writing). By tapping into search data furnished by their cloud infrastructure providers, they can incorporate search data for the term "solar panels" and use it as part of a model to predict supply and demand of the solar energy market. In a business environment where price is no longer a differentiator, speed becomes the dependent variable.

Wilson and his leadership team can measure how long each user spends in a tool, time spent setting up a template, running an event, the efficacy of a category blueprint, and the average time per project. All this data is sitting right there at the touch of the screen.

Tools

Wilson is very pragmatic about what does and doesn't work in tooling. He and other leaders of his generation wear the scars from overhyped, overpromised, and overinflated delusions of technical grandeur that failed spectacularly. As he notes, big bets on tooling lock you into multiyear if not decades-long investments where changing course is next to impossible. For the VPC journey they started with a strategic decision to build off a cloud infrastructure. Next they layered on their legacy platforms (those with many years of depreciation left). Then they've added a series of point solutions to give them the necessary functionality that the larger platforms lack. Having a cohesive and integrated technology stack gives them the ability to surface and exchange data across the entire supply chain and with their third parties in real time. That allows them to build control towers (and eventually digital twins) infused with real-time data and intelligence. This alone is a remarkable achievement and should be applauded. However, this is what they have already accomplished; what they're in the process of building will be truly spectacular.

Once VPC had the proper cloud platform and digital tooling in place (and good underlying data), the question of automation started to emerge. Could they start to automate their non-strategic sourcing and contracting activities? Could they create an automated bot to evaluate suppliers, set up sourcing events, score tenders, sign contracts, and put them into the core systems? Thus Ava was born.[126]

Ava is designed to be an automated, intelligent bot capable of executing sourcing events (RFPs, auctions, and so on) and contracting activities. The bot is architected to incorporate the category strategy (preferred suppliers, commercial models) while including supplier collaboration and stakeholder alignment. All this will take place with little or no direct manual involvement from procurement. They've gone on to include other autonomous capabilities such as supplier discovery, data enrichment, and intelligent process orchestration (individually personalized, unique user experiences created through generative AI).

---

[126] According to Sabih Rozales, Ava is not an acronym, but rather was the name chosen by the collective team, by way of a survey. Ava is the name of the robot main character featured in the 2014 movie *Ex Machina*. The choice to assign a name was an attempt to humanize the bot.

Regardless of how the Ava journey plays out, the entire organization will have learned a tremendous amount about what is possible and what is practical in terms of automating supply chain and procurement activities. By taking this journey, they're positioned to embrace the power of generative AI because they possess the foundational platforms, point solutions, and data.

People

In my interview with Wilson, he made three comments that struck me as the essence of being a good digital leader. First, he wants to be at the leading edge for himself. He wants to be surrounded by smart people doing cool things with digital so he can learn and benefit from it. This sounds so obvious and yet VPC is among a very select few operating like this. Second, he loves it when one can take data and visualize it. That comment was laced with intellectual curiosity. It's easy to imagine Wilson's excitement when people bring new data sources or insights to him. Third, failure is embraced, not punished. Written on company coffee mugs is the message: "It's ~~not~~ okay to make mistakes." This sets for employees a cultural tone of exploration and endeavor, where the journey is as important as the destination. (See Figure 20: *Vodafone Procurement Company mugs* on page 182.)

The most important person in the room

I sat in on various meetings throughout my time at VPC. However, I was struck by a particular moment during a random development meeting for the Ava autonomous procurement project. The meeting participants consisted of developers and business users jointly designing the solution. At one point, both teams got stuck and the developers became fixated on the technical capabilities and limitations. Meanwhile, the business users were getting confused and quickly losing interest in the technical minutiae. This lack of understanding is exactly where internal development projects rotate off their axis and begin a slow trajectory to crash and burn. Alas, that didn't happen because a gentleman by the name of Sabih Rozales, the business architect (at the time), interjected and righted the ship. He did a masterful job holding space for the technical team while translating technical issues into business-friendly language. This technical-to-business (and reverse) translator was the most important person that day and for just about every other successful corporate development project. As you might expect, these people are hard to find because they have a highly developed understanding

Figure 20
Vodafone Procurement Company mugs

Source: Elouise Epstein

of the business, technical acumen, and the ability to relate to multiple audiences simultaneously. Watching Rozales successfully steer the project in that small moment made me wonder how many instances like that he has mediated (or will successfully mediate) over the course of the project.

In my experience and through observations of corporate digital initiatives, far too often enterprises substitute non-technical project managers in lieu of highly skilled translators like Rozales. Predictably this leads to much management activity with very little technical success. This is because without finely attenuated technical mediation, the non-technical business users quickly get overwhelmed under the fusillade of jargon and "quiet quit" the project. This opens the way for the technical people to push through what is the most expedient solution so they can complete their milestones. All the while the project manager is dutifully checking off milestones on the Gantt chart, blissfully unaware that the initiative has derailed. The net result is a subpar solution that has little relevance to the business and certainly will never be confused for transformational.

Of course, the challenge is to find more people like Rozales who have these unique and eclectic skills. Finding them may be hard, but not as impossible as it once was now that we have had several generations of people working for the big tech companies that have matriculated into the corporate workforce. The key is to attract them by giving them autonomy and cool tools. As Wilson points out, if you don't invest in these resources and make them feel loved, they won't sign on or stay. (See Sidebar: *The teardown lab* on page 184.)

Final observations

I left Luxembourg moved by three observations. First, thinking back to the deficit perspective applied to procurement (as noted in Chapter X, *Building digitally savvy supply chain leadership*) that accuses supply chain practitioners who "don't have the data, are hard to work with, and implicitly need consultants and tech providers." Looking at what VPC has achieved, it's clear that most perceptions of practitioners are outdated and wrong. Wilson and his team are not dependent on consultants or tech software providers to run their business successfully. This allows them to choose when and where they bring in outside help versus being dependent on it. This has

The teardown lab

I spent my day in a corner conference room at the VPC headquarters. In the next room was their teardown lab (TL). While interviewing this team was not my objective, I was treated to an in-depth discussion with the two people who created and run this capability. The pessimist in me was initially underwhelmed by this prospect; it seems like everyone has a TL (even Kearney does).[127] After an hour with them, I realized that having a TL built into the company's fabric allowed for insights to be piped directly to the category managers, who can use the information to adjust or inform category management strategies. Connecting the TL engineers to the category managers and the business has a very noticeable effect in creating comfort with data, technology, and business need. In short, this duo were describing how they were using tools and intelligence to change how VPC people operate.

In their early days, it took them two to three weeks to do a printed circuit board cost breakdown, which required using an actual magnifying glass to read the individual embedded components. Now they have a very sophisticated scanner that digitizes and tracks all the components, building a bottom-up bill of materials. This database of products and commodities allows them to track changes over time. Also, it gives them the ability to track the evolution of technological changes and new manufacturing techniques. Most importantly, when suppliers increase costs in response to market changes (say, the price of memory spikes), they can quickly validate if this is a legitimate increase. This is directly actionable data. It also gives the category managers and VPC the leverage to look at remanufacturing particular products with a contract manufacturer. Moreover, all this data at their fingertips gives them interesting insights into ESG and risk. They showed me a recently torn-down router that was supposedly made in Ireland. But upon closer inspection, the router had American chips manufactured in China, assembled in Germany, and sent to Ireland for final assembly. Lots of ESG overhead for that router, not to mention risk. This allows VPC greater visibility into a product's provenance, something that the collection of third parties may not be willing or able to share.

---

[127] I would be remiss (and perhaps reprimanded) if I don't point out that Kearney's teardown lab (Product Excellence and Renewal Lab or PERLab) is really a design-to-value lab that brings together product design, development, engineering, sustainability, user experience, and manufacturing experts to take a holistic view of the product life cycle.

the advantage of setting up mutually beneficial tech partnerships (for example, their cloud provider).

VPC is not scared of failure. Wilson has set an ambitious digital agenda and makes it clear that failure is an important learning tool. When failures occur, he and the team weather them together. Finally, just to demonstrate how prepared the folks at VPC are for the boom, I was sitting alone in the conference room when the fire alarm went off. This was not a planned test. I was unsure what to do and my shock at the situation kicked in (definitely not my best moment). I peeked out the door down the hallway, and it was empty; everyone had exited the building. After a few moments of hesitation, I grabbed my phone and jacket to make my way out. Just then, two people from Rozales' team came to collect me. They had the situational awareness both to know that I was in the building and to ensure I got out. I was touched and impressed by this act. When the boom occurs, how do people respond? In this case, the fire alarm turned out to be a malfunction, but it showed exactly how people who are prepared act in moments of crisis. This is an apt metaphor for how VPC approaches business.

Hacking corporate culture: five takeaways to VPC's digital success

— Hire the right people, give them autonomy, cool tools, and get out of the way.

— Investing in digital conveys love and appreciation, and if you don't then the talent won't stay.

— Hire people with the intention that they'll be so successful they'll go to Google in three years—this is a win.

— Ensure you have the most important person present in the room.

— Embrace mistakes and failure.

Chapter XIII
Stepping off the edge to the future

> **"Computers are useless. They can only give you answers."**
>
> **– Pablo Picasso**

We've traversed a lot of territory regarding the risks facing supply chains, the roles that intelligence, tools, and people play in securing and optimizing supply chains, and why a new approach to digital is crucial. Yet, when it comes to knowing what's next—and what will most disrupt future chains—we're all still reading the tea leaves. However, our ability to be ready for the change is paramount, even as we're determining what that change will be.

Attack of the machines

I have established the layering roles of intelligence, tools, and people. But in this era of "AI," what happens when the machines learn how to attack? I have argued so far that we need to start operating like hackers, which means constantly trying to find vulnerabilities in our supply chains. We need to attempt to break them, fix them, and run this exercise over and over again. But that is labor and capital intensive. What if I could instead teach a machine to look for vulnerabilities repeatedly and endlessly? This is not science fiction. For the past few years, China has held a number of robot hacking games, where contestants bring AI/ML tools to work autonomously or in hybrid partnership with humans to attack systems. There have been human versions of these contests for years.[128]

---

[128] Schneier, Bruce. "AIs as Computer Hackers." Schneier on Security, February 2, 2023. https://www.schneier.com/blog/archives/2023/02/ais-as-computer-hackers.html (Accessed May 11, 2023).

The emergence of machine-against-machine contests is truly staggering and ups the ante. To let a machine autonomously run testing on known vulnerabilities and then predict and learn new vulnerabilities is scary. If ChatGPT can code an application, then it can be used to scan an application and find its vulnerabilities. This is truly a hacking force multiplier.

Every time we talk about the impact of machine learning, we have to understand how it can be hacked. The term is known as model inversion. Hackers can reverse-engineer algorithms to get the system to expose the underlying training data. With the underlying data exposed, our nefarious characters can then exploit the algorithms for their own gains. This is using the machine learning system as intended but for unintended purposes.[129]

Before we panic, these same tools and approaches can be used to secure systems. My question is, are you ready? Are your supply chain systems up to the task? More importantly, are you ready for the ensuing chaos this will bring?

Pandemic risk management lessons

Historians, scholars, and political leaders (we hope) will spend the next century studying the causes, responses, and lessons learned from the COVID-19 pandemic. Never has a global society had so many means and resources to identify, prepare, prevent, contain, and eliminate disease, and yet failed so spectacularly. The lack of adequate PPE, ventilators, data collection, testing capabilities, or consistent prevention methods led to a global tragedy. The fact that pharmaceutical companies and scientists developed a vaccine in such a short time is a testament to the triumph of the human spirit. As we move from pandemic to endemic, there are some very uncomfortable questions.

Leaving out the political aspects of the COVID-19 discussion (masking, vaccine mandates, government authority, vaccine equality, and so on) and without getting into a broader critique of public health, there are a few practical areas of the pandemic response that should sound familiar to every supply chain practitioner. Pulitzer Prize winner and staff writer at *The Atlantic* Ed Yong points

---

[129] Schneier, Bruce. "Attacking Machine Learning Systems." Schneier on Security, February 6, 2023. https://www.schneier.com/blog/archives/2023/02/attacking-machine-learning-systems.html (Accessed May 11, 2023).

out multiple issues: we have built a society that is intensely vulnerable to health crises; public health data is difficult to collect, process, and analyze; and very little effort is put into disease prevention and control. I could write that same statement about today's supply chains and it would be nearly identical: we have built a [supply chain] that is intensely vulnerable to [disruptions]; [supply chain] data is difficult to collect, process, and analyze; and very little effort is put into prevention and control. In fact, that is a central thesis of this book.

We have to get much better at collecting third-party data and turning it into intelligence that we can use to feed digital tools that make supply chain practitioners more effective, and supply chains more secure.

Yong also suggests that we need to get better at designing our society to be more tolerant to health crises: for example, making high-quality ventilation for buildings, improving testing frequency and collection, and upgrading hospitals. Or, more succinctly, he points out that he can pull out his phone and it will tell him whether it will rain in a micro location. So why can't we know whether there's a spike in an infectious disease or other public health consideration in the same place? Of course, it requires integrating many proprietary legacy systems across government agencies and even countries. Plus, we would need to add vastly more data collection and distribution capabilities so that we can ingest the data and deliver it in a timely fashion (a gigantic data governance headache). If this sounds familiar, it's exactly what we need to do to build the next-generation supply chain. Ethics notwithstanding, the only difference is that there is neither the political will nor money to do this for public health. However, there's plenty of money and will to do this for global supply chains. Ultimately, we had several opportunities to stop the pandemic, but that would have required pulling out all the stops—something that was politically, culturally, and socially impossible.[130]

Similarly, when it comes to threats to our supply chains, an unwillingness to share information with your third parties and other industries keeps everyone

---

[130] Yong, Ed. "How the Pandemic Will End." *The Atlantic*, March 20, 2020. https://www.theatlantic.com/health/archive/2020/03/how-will-coronavirus-end/608719/ (Accessed May 11, 2023).
"Science Journalist Ed Yong on the Future of the Pandemic." KQED, July 16, 2020. https://www.kqed.org/forum/2010101878685/science-journalist-ed-yong-on-the-future-of-the-pandemic (Accessed May 11, 2023).

equally at risk. One company's unwillingness or inability to secure their industrial control systems, stop accepting emailed invoices, or not let others know when they've been breached keeps the exploits in circulation. One infected device will continually look for other vulnerable devices in which to spread its virus. You may be secure today, but if you slip, then that virus, malware, ransomware from the infected device will attack. These attacks target systems that do not use logic; these programs are binary. So collectively we need to design and patch our systems to ensure that devices can't be infected and that the viruses simply fade into the ethereal dustbin.

The next disruption

As a futurist, the question people most often ask me is, what is the next big disruption? It's a hard question for anyone to answer, and nobody can truly know the future with any certainty; at least I can't. Will it be another pandemic? Possibly. Will it be a huge cyberattack? Probably. Will it be a nuclear war? Hopefully not. These disruptions and the countless others that occupy the daily news cycle are what we know. What I like to look at is the slow-moving, seemingly micro-impact trends that are occurring and what they mean more broadly. The "lying flat" phenomenon in China is noteworthy but hardly a cause for alarm. Same thing for the work-from-home trend. In the US, we have the student loan debt crisis, gun violence, social inequality, and environmental destruction.

In this context, perhaps the next greatest disruption is confronting the limits of a capitalistic global society.

I think one of the greatest future supply chain disruptions might be a recalibration of capitalism—or at least parts of it. I know I am about to lose 75 percent of readers but don't go just yet. This is not a liberal treatise on why capitalism is deleterious or an advocation for some other system (socialism, imperialism, monarchy, oligarchy, or religious state). It's merely to point out that if we're going to imagine and design tomorrow's supply chain, we have to take a critical look at the underlying political and social systems upon which our supply chains will operate. During the pandemic lockdown people survived with less. We took up gardening, breadmaking, household repairs, and other such activities when supply of goods was low and free time was aplenty. The breakneck pace of consumption that the global economy is based upon has side effects, whether human or environmental. As supply chain designers and managers, it's incumbent upon us to ask if there is a future whereby consumption drops precipitously due to societal factors.

Everybody in leadership today is making decisions for the next generation without the benefit of knowing how society will evolve, just as leaders in the late 1990s and early 2000s did when they moved operations across the globe in pursuit of the lowest cost. I'm not judging those decisions—just pointing out that we have a choice to make, and we will be judged in future decades. As supply chain designers, we assume that capitalism and technological progress are inevitable, but are they?

The underlying premise of today's supply chain designs assumes ever-increasing levels of consumption. Accordingly, job one is to get any product to any place in the world within a matter of hours as cheaply as possible. We have proven we can do that, but it's not clear whether our global societies will be able to sustain this. What happens when we don't go rushing out for the next great consumer digital device? What happens when people decide that microplastics or chemicals entering our body through nonstick cookware is not what we want? What if one of the lessons from the pandemic is that we need to move from toilet paper to bidets? What if we move from highly consumable products (like fast fashion), which have a heavier dependence on supply chains running without disruption, to more precise, long-lasting products? I'm not advocating any of this, but merely pointing out how these trends would affect tomorrow's supply chains. Otherwise, we're simply setting our new supply chain to be upended by events and dynamics out of our control.

Imagine that you go into a clothing store, you head for the T-shirt section, and you have two options: T-shirt one was made with child slave labor and T-shirt two was not made with child slave labor. Which would you choose? I'm guessing (hoping) you'd choose the one not made with child slave labor.[131] So why do all of us completely disregard the immense pain, suffering, and

---

[131] Ironclad. "The Hidden Bloodshed Of EVs, Cobalt Mining, & Modern Slavery (w/ Siddharth Kara)." YouTube video, 39:31. March 28, 2023. https://www.youtube.com/watch?v=0viUxUS21Oc (Accessed May 28, 2023).

environmental destruction in cobalt mining? Everyone who uses a smartphone, laptop, drives an electric vehicle, or any other device with a rechargeable battery is contributing to the exploitation and forced labor of thousands of women and children. As Siddharth Kara points out in his groundbreaking study *Cobalt Red: How the Blood of the Congo Powers our Lives,* cobalt is the key mineral that enables portable batteries to have long lives without overheating. Nearly 75 percent of cobalt comes from the Democratic Republic of Congo. The mining there is done in horribly unsafe conditions. Cobalt is highly toxic to breathe in or touch and yet thousands, including women with babies, mine it without proper tools (often with bare hands), protection, compensation, or basic human rights. In many cases armed soldiers force the labor.

Essentially, the multitrillion-dollar tech market and the rapidly exploding electric vehicle (EV) market, both extraordinarily profitable industries, extract profits on the backs of the poorest citizens. While there are many sustainable mining initiatives and you might be thinking, "not my favorite tech company," the reality is that at the bottom of the supply chain ethically mined cobalt is mixed with blood-soaked cobalt (a problem palm oil production suffers from). When you get on the ground, as Kara did (access is limited and highly dangerous), you will find a problem that defies modern conceptions of human decency. Yet we possess an unending appetite for more and more rechargeable batteries. We're so wedded to our smartphones (and laptops) to conduct our lives, and EVs are a crucial component of our global decarbonization efforts, it's hard to imagine that demand for cobalt will abate anytime soon.[132]

So the question is, now that we know, do we continue the never-ending quest for portable technological sophistication at the expense of society's most vulnerable, causing untold suffering? This is where unbridled demand and deep supply chain visibility may present some limits to our assumptions about capitalism. It will be changing consumer habits that will first bring about changes to demand. Undoubtedly regulations will follow thereafter. So as we design the next-generation supply chain, we need to be aware of those consuming at the top and those laboring at the bottom. We should also ask ourselves: How much technology do we really need?

---

[132] Siddharth, Kara. *Cobalt Red: How the Blood of the Congo Powers Our Lives* (New York: St. Martin's Press, 2023).

Peak digital?

When is there too much digital? I know this is ironic for a digital futurist to ask, especially when I started this book by discussing the problems with a paper-based vaccine record. But it's a question we must continually consider.

Alarms are being raised about the digital security of today's automobiles. Web security researcher Sam Curry states, "Nearly every automobile manufactured in the last five years had nearly identical functionality. If an attacker were able to find vulnerabilities in the API endpoints that vehicle telematics systems used, they could honk the horn, flash the lights, remotely track, lock/unlock, and start/stop vehicles completely remotely." So he and his friends decided to test out their theory. Their results were staggering and scary. They identified vulnerabilities in Kia, Honda, Infiniti, Nissan, Acura, Hyundai, and Genesis cars, allowing them to fully remote lock, unlock, engine-start, engine-stop, precision locate, flash headlights, and honk vehicles using only the victim's email address. Due to misconfigured single sign-on, this group could create their own accounts on Mercedes-Benz internal systems, giving them full documentation and source code to the Mercedes app. Shockingly, once they had legitimate credentials and access to the internal Slack system, they could have easily elevated their privileges (as happened in the Twitter hack). Fortunately, these hackers submitted their findings to Mercedes-Benz admins, but the response they received was less than reassuring. This is likely because (and I am guessing here) the Mercedes-Benz admins weren't used to dealing with third parties submitting security issues.[133] Interestingly, I had a similar experience with American Express years ago when I came across a website error that exposed some confidential security information. I tried to report it to their admins, who didn't understand and thus dismissed it. A perfect example of humans' greatest deficiency—the ego.

If we look more closely at these automotive digital security lapses, many originate at the weakest point: between the manufacturer and the dealers (third parties). My hypothesis is that the security weakness creeps in where the manufacturer has to connect and integrate with thousands of dealers, many

---

[133] Curry, Sam. "Web Hackers vs. the Auto Industry." Sam Curry, January 3, 2023. https://samcurry.net/web-hackers-vs-the-auto-industry/ (Accessed May 11, 2023).

of whom may not be as digitally savvy as they need to be. However, since there's a greater focus on the customer experience of car performance, securing communication with the dealers probably takes a back seat. Again, the third party is the weak link.

The right to repair

In March 2020, Vice News produced a video entitled *Farmers Are Hacking Their Tractors Because of a Repair Ban,* which featured the lengths farmers were going to so that they could fix their tractors. This included downloading hacked versions of John Deere software from Eastern Europe. In what is becoming an altogether refrain from the digital age, people, businesses, and even the military buy expensive, complicated equipment that runs proprietary software. But when the equipment stops working, even for minor issues, only a dealer is authorized to repair it. Loading up a massive tractor and having it hauled hundreds of miles simply to have a John Deere service technician connect a computer and update some software or clear a fault seems ridiculous, not to mention costly. Even worse, what happens when the manufacturer stops supporting a particular module or feature? This forces the customer to upgrade or not use the feature, which can be problematic.

Vice News's video basically asks why it is that a farmer, or any of us really, can't have access to the underlying software to fix problems. Especially considering how these disruptions can have deleterious effects on farmers' ability to effectively do their job and feed the nation and world. Farmers were able to do this in the predigital age, so why not now? To punctuate this point, the Vice News video ends by showing a farmer's old tractors juxtaposed against the brand-new digitally enabled tractors. He points out that the old tractors still work after 100 years, and muses whether these new tractors will still be working in 100 years.

As of January 9, 2023, John Deere changed its policy and granted US farmers the right to repair their equipment without using proprietary parts and service facilities. In exchange, representatives for the farmers have agreed not to push for state or federal right-to-repair regulations.[134] This acquiescence by John

---

[134] Krok, Andrew. "Farmers are hacking their tractors so they can actually fix them." CNET, March 22, 2017. https://www.cnet.com/roadshow/news/farmers-using-hacked-firmware-to-bypass-john-deeres-software-stranglehold/ (Accessed May 11, 2023).

Deere shows just how much weight the farmers' voices carried in this fight. When the food supply is threatened, people (especially politicians) take notice. But the right-to-repair (R2R) movement is just starting.

If you're a fan of McDonald's, you're probably painfully aware that on any given visit there's a decent chance the ice cream machine is broken. The problem is so pervasive it has become a meme, a popular TikTok, and was a joke on *The Daily Show* with Trevor Noah.[135] Twenty-four-year-old Rashiq Zahid built mcbroken.com to track which locations have an out-of-order machine, using a bot to place an order for ice cream at every McDonald's every 30 minutes. According to Wired, anywhere from five to 16 percent of ice cream machines are broken at any given time.[136] As I write, I checked mcbroken, and right now 12 percent of Bay Area ice cream machines are down, while 27 percent in San Diego, and 27 percent in New York are currently out of order. The issue has become so bad that the US Federal Trade Commission has investigated.

How could such a successful business continually fail to deliver for its customers, readily lose revenue, and open itself up for a public thrashing by its competitors? The answer lies at the intersection of R2R, third-party management, and hacking. Taylor, a company specializing in "commercial soft serve, frozen beverage and commercial griddles" supplies digital ice cream machines to tens of thousands of McDonald's restaurants globally. Of course, Taylor has deemed the equipment and software of the machine as proprietary, allowing only approved distributors to service the equipment. Thus, you have a poorly performing machine, frequently out of service, and no matter how simple the solution to fix the problem, you have to wait hours or days for a Taylor authorized technician to come out. Much like the John Deere situation, McDonald's franchisees are unable to sell a popular item and lose money accordingly due to an inability to contract or do their own maintenance. It's

---

[135] Competitor Jack in the Box trolled McDonald's by creating a viral TikTok poking fun at the ice cream machine debacle.
Tyko, Kelly. "Jack In the Box trolls McDonald's broken ice cream machines to promote new Oreo mint shake." USATODAY, March 3, 2022. https://www.usatoday.com/story/money/food/2022/03/03/mcdonalds-jack-in-box-ice-cream-mcbroken/9357329002/ (Accessed May 11, 2023).

[136] According to Wired, *The website McBroken.com, which uses a bot to automatically attempt to place an online order for ice cream at every McDonald's in America every 20 to 30 minutes and measures the results, reveals that at any given time over the past two months, somewhere between 5 and 16 percent of all US McDonald's are unable to sell ice cream.*
Greenberg, Andy. "They Hacked McDonald's Ice Cream Makers—and Started a Cold War." Wired, April 20, 2021. https://www.wired.com/story/they-hacked-mcdonalds-ice-cream-makers-started-cold-war/ (Accessed May 11, 2023).

even worse when the issue might be as simple as when the machine was cleaned (which happens every night), something may not have been put back together properly. Franchisee owners need to wait days and pay hundreds of dollars for a Taylor technician to tell them that was the issue.

Innovators and entrepreneurs Jeremy O'Sullivan and Melissa Nelson realized that you can "press the cone icon on the screen of the Taylor C602 digital ice cream machine … then tap the buttons that show a snowflake and a milkshake to set the digits on the screen to 5, then 2, then 3, then 1. After that precise series of no fewer than 16 button presses, a menu magically unlocks … with this cheat code you can access the machine's vital signs." Realizing the utility of making the machine's internal operations easily accessible, they created a gadget and company called Kytch. The device sits within the machine, monitors all the internal workings, and presents any error messages along with suggested fixes. A very clever and useful hack. Going back to the use case described above, if a franchisee owner or manager can see that a machine didn't finish its sanitize cycle because it wasn't reassembled properly after cleaning, then they can solve the issue before business opens. It eliminates the need for a service repair call. After initially being supportive of the idea, eventually Taylor and by extension McDonald's allegedly reverse-engineered the Kytch device, created their own device, and then forbade franchisees from using Kytch or any other third party. Eventually Kytch went out of business and now there is ongoing litigation.[137]

The Kytch story is both a useful and cautionary tale. If we think about it from an intelligence–tools–people point of view, there are some useful correlations. First, what franchisees lacked was intelligence about the inner workings and potential problems of their ice cream machines. It was pretty easy for O'Sullivan and Nelson to build a tool to create the intelligence. Giving the intelligence to franchisee owners/managers became a huge operational lift. It should have been a win for all parties: Kytch, franchisee owners, employees, McDonald's, and Taylor. Is this not what innovation is all about? Taylor and McDonald's heavy-handed response demonstrated that they viewed the problem in analog terms. Like John Deere did initially, they treated their

[137] Greenberg, Andy. "They Hacked McDonald's Ice Cream Makers—and Started a Cold War." Wired, April 20, 2021. https://www.wired.com/story/they-hacked-mcdonalds-ice-cream-makers-started-cold-war/ (Accessed May 11, 2023).

machine as a black box only openable by them. But, in the digital age, nothing is a closed box.

When farmers acquire John Deere software from Eastern Europe it begs all kinds of questions and concerns, not least of which is the provenance of the software. Does this contain malware that could be propagated to other networked tractors and executed later down the line, bringing all tractors in the US to a halt? It could be a ransomware attack at best or turn the tractor into a weapon of destruction at worst. What's worse for Taylor is that Kytch demonstrated the machine's poor digital security. What John Deere and Taylor should have done is provided a software developer kit and a community around repairing machines, which meant they could control and have visibility into how people were using and solving problems (and then fixed said problems). Instead they took an analog approach, that of putting profits over any other broader concerns. Moreover, these decisions must have been made by people who didn't understand the implications of building and maintaining digital devices, especially in non-technology industries. Again, this brings to the fore: Where do intellectual property rights start and stop?

The risk that keeps me up at night

Perhaps the greatest threat to our supply chains will be the humans who run them.

Every corporation suffers from human fallibility. This is just an observation, not a criticism. Turf wars over ownership, reporting structure, and political capital are just many of the day-to-day issues that plague large enterprises— this on top of highly matrixed and complicated op models and governance structures that not only stifle innovation but also day-to-day operations. Sometimes there's simply a culture of mistrust among different functions, business units, or even between executives. Then there are the middle managers, who act as a bridge between leaders and rank-and-file employees. It is the middle managers who continually sandbag digital transformations. Case in point: I have a client that's struggling with the rollout of a subpar contract management system and process. The middle manager tasked with the project is content to keep rolling it out indefinitely. There is little motivation to do more than conduct meetings to talk about deployment. And, when they do deploy it is a soft deployment, where the tool is made available and the "training" is done, but adoption is left to the individual end user's preference. Not so shockingly, the result is a continuation of the status quo. The middle manager knows full well that meeting their annual performance objectives is tied to the activity of rollout and not successful adoption. When pushed, this middle manager went on a long rant about the dangers of deploying an untested technology and assured everyone that there was nothing to worry about. This reflexive defensiveness to such a monumental pain point is a clear example of how middle managers do as little as possible while hiding behind any plausible excuse for inaction. Interestingly, after that meeting a junior person on the team reached out to me on LinkedIn and was very engaged and excited about the future. Finally, there is need for greater digital literacy within any enterprise's leadership team. This means that there is a collective knowledge and empowerment versus simply deferring all things technology to the CIO.

The incomparable Steve Jobs, speaking to the Santa Clara Valley Historical Association in 1994, stated, "The minute you understand that you can poke life and actually something will, you know if you push in, something will pop out the other side, that you can change it, you can mold it. That's maybe the most important thing. It's to shake off this erroneous notion that life is there and you're just gonna live in it, versus embrace it, change it, improve it, make your mark upon it."[138] Jobs was encouraging people to live their best lives by not accepting the constraints of what is, but instead to imagine and create what could be. By poking, prodding, changing, life can be improved. He was urging people to refuse to accept things as they are by opening them up, taking them apart, and putting them back together in a different way. In short, he was suggesting for individuals to hack society's expectations and chart their own course. This is no different than what we as supply chain professionals need to do.

In the digital and information age, innovations and breakthroughs happen at a lightning pace. Today's best practice is tomorrow's blunder. Today's supplier is tomorrow's competitor. Today's competitor is tomorrow's partner.

[138] Silicon Valley Historical Association. "Steve Jobs Secrets of Life." YouTube video, 1:39. October 6, 2011. https://www.youtube.com/watch?v=kYfNvmF0Bqw (Accessed May 11, 2023).

The better we get at managing our relationships and using the associated data exchange and corresponding digital capabilities, the better chance we will have at successfully securing and building resilient supply chains. My challenge to today's supply chain leaders: Will you be a steward of the enterprise? Will you make the tough choices and go against the CIO if necessary? Will you inspire folks to build something better? Will you measure progress without change, activity instead of productivity? How do you want your tenure to be evaluated by future generations? Were you the one who bought the big ERP system that cost $1 billion, took a decade to implement, and was out of date the day you signed the contract? Sure, you did your job and nobody will hold you accountable when it fails to meet the promises of expectations. But is that the legacy you want to leave? Even if CEOs and board members don't understand the importance of what we do, the world is watching and future business leaders will judge the choices we make today. We are at a once-in-a-generation moment as supply chain professionals. Will we embrace it? If not us, then who? And if not now, when?

My sincere hope is that by the time the next global health crisis comes around we will be able to get proper medical resources (vaccine, medical device, whatever) to everyone who needs it. I for one am tired of putting products into my body where I can't see where it was manufactured, how it was handled, and what route it took to get to me. My expectation is that collectively we will start to receive provenance and track-and-trace data for everything we consume, whether it's a bag of pretzels or a tablet computer. As supply chain practitioners and leaders, this is the promise we must make to society. And nobody had better ask me to store crucial information on a piece of paper ever again.

Chapter XIV
Afterword

"If you're over 30, I don't care what you have to say about GenAI."

– Elouise Epstein

The hardest part about writing this book, aside from my propensity for distraction, was knowing when to stop writing and say I was done with it. Writing a practitioner-focused book when the world is changing is difficult. Knowing when to stop is impossible. The explosion of ChatGPT (and Google's Bard) severely tested my ability to finish this book. While I've managed to incorporate some examples within these pages, there's so much more to say on the subject, hence my need to write an afterword on the implications. As a futurist it is so tempting to prognosticate about where we're going. Instead, what I would like to focus on is how this new technology will affect the risk and resilience of our supply chains.

There's no doubt we have hit a monumental milestone in the mainstream acceptance and usage of AI.

Between the visual media generators and the fierce competition among the large tech players, we're at a seminal moment in technological development and witnessing the transition from the Information Age to the Artificial Intelligence Age.

Another "Amazon.com" moment

For the past decade, procurement practitioners have been struggling against the Amazon comparison. Users have joined a chorus of complaints bemoaning, "Why isn't the corporate buying experience like Amazon.com?" Variations of this complaint have reverberated throughout the corporate halls for almost a decade now. Users are unwilling to endure painful buying experiences at work when they have an infinitely better buying experience on Amazon.com at home. This has put CPOs and their teams and the whole ProcureTech ecosystem on notice that users are dissatisfied (a phenomenon I have written about extensively in my previous books).

We're having another of these moments, not just for procurement, but for the entire enterprise (and our personal lives). "Just ChatGPT it" is the phrase I keep hearing. While it's early days, it feels that the ease of use and sophistication of ChatGPT will further cast a shadow over the bevy of complicated, unusable, trash corporate systems. At the top of that list will be ERP systems.

So how do we think about ChatGPT in the context of the future of supply chain systems? First, we must remember that no matter how great ChatGPT is, right now it is an audience of one. You enter your input and receive an output personalized to you, which is great except that you are the audience. You are still responsible for the shaping and dissemination of that content. If everyone's using ChatGPT, then how do you stand out? We run the risk of groupthink at a mega scale (consider the resilience whitepaper problem). This is how those who understand and can wield the power of ChatGPT creatively will stand out.

I was at a recent partner meeting and we had a guest speaker give a ChatGPT 101. You could feel the collective panic when the partners realized that junior consultants use ChatGPT regularly for client work. Very few partners in the room were familiar with the tool, how it works, or the risks. Again, here we have an example where rank-and-file employees are using technology that the leaders don't fully understand.

To solve this gap in digital literacy, I urged our leadership to embrace the principles elucidated in Chapter VI, *Hacking AI and building algorithmic literacy* at our next partner meeting. Specifically, I want every single partner (including myself) to learn ChatGPT by using it to solve problems that are personal to them. I want them to fail at it repeatedly. I want all of us to sit in a room together, sharing what we're learning, shortcuts, watchouts, and even jailbreaks. I want everyone to leave the next partner meeting reflecting on what they did and didn't learn. The more we use these tools, the more relevant they are to us as individuals, the more we share our learnings with one another, the more we fail with our queries, and the more we will learn. For the record, there's no need for a corporate training program to learn ChatGPT. Although by the time this book is published, there will undoubtedly be many of them.

Business is about two (or more) parties coming together to buy and sell goods and services. Ultimately this involves a relationship between the parties. AI will enhance the negotiating, contracting, reporting, compliance, and countless other menial tasks, but ultimately business strategy will continue to be governed by market forces, government regulations, consumer demand, employee capabilities, and supplier capabilities. AI will not completely replace those activities (at least not for the next decade), so we must retain a strong focus on solid business foundations and principles. While that may seem obvious, amid the chaos and hype surrounding ChatGPT, a huge risk is that we will lose sight of business fundamentals. More to the point for supply chains, we must not forget that to effectively run a next-generation supply chain, we have to get good at exchanging data with a wide variety of third parties. Then we must turn that data into intelligence and, in some cases, share it freely.

Finally, no matter how great AI is today or becomes tomorrow, we are humans living in a physical world (at least until our AI overlords take physical form and turn on us). For the foreseeable future, AI will help us work faster, smarter, expand our capabilities, and do whatever else it will eventually do. Meanwhile, the sun will rise and set each day. We will continue to engage with our family and friends. And successful business will continue to boil down to relationships between the company, employee, supplier, customer, government, and other assorted third parties. So I encourage everyone reading this to spend as much time as possible embracing your humanity; it's the one thing that AI can't replicate. Develop your relationship skills as much as your AI knowledge. More importantly, embrace the human experience. Take a hike, watch the sunset at the Pacific Ocean, give someone a hug (consensually), or simply look up into the vastness of the universe on a clear night and contemplate the beauty of our world.

Index

Index (continued)

Index (continued)

Index (continued)

Index (continued)

Index (continued)

Index (continued)

Index (continued)

Index (continued)

Index (continued)

Index

Index (continued)

Index (continued)

Bonus chapter
Improving security and resilience through supplier experience management

"We are digital property being sold."

– Sean Hamam, executive chauffeur and head of operations

Why your suppliers hate your company

As if forcing suppliers to use archaic EDI technology wasn't bad enough, it gets worse. Traditional thinking and so-called best practices have given us many buyer-focused procurement and supply chain systems. Buyers and the business users they serve are the consumers of these sourcing, contracting, requisitioning, and payment systems. Hence there's a natural bias toward making these systems appealing to whomever writes the check. To put it more succinctly: we have lived in a buyer-centric world focused entirely on serving internal business stakeholders. As a result, our systems and the data that underpin them are all about making procurement more efficient and better able to support the business. Although that's a laudable objective, it leaves the largest constituency—suppliers—unrepresented.

Nearly every ERP, S2P, and P2P system (and even many point solution systems) treats suppliers as a commodity—assuming they will jump over whatever hurdles are necessary. The underlying rationale is that suppliers want the business, so they will engage no matter what. Both the underlying premise and the practical application put the buyers on a pedestal. Nowhere is this more obvious than the dreaded supplier portal. For example, let's say Acme Company launches a new S2P system. Part of the implementation involves setting up Acme's supplier portal, which will serve as the one and only point of access for suppliers. In theory, this portal concept sounds good, but it creates a logic trap in the design and a dumpster fire in the deployment.

The illogicalness of a supplier portal becomes clear when you put yourself in the supplier's shoes. Suddenly you're confronted with the stark reality of the effort a supplier has to put into entering and consuming information from the portal. Now imagine that supplier replicating that onerous process for every single one of its customers' supplier portals. Even worse, nearly all portals lack a cohesive, integrated, and up-to-date place for useful information. Instead, they are simply launching points to other systems—as many as a dozen. There is often no integration, no common user experience, and no common user interface. Shockingly, sometimes core functionality isn't even there. This is true for nearly every procurement supplier portal. All of this leads to what Gartner terms "portal fatigue." Moreover, companies continue to burden their suppliers with countless initiatives, including those focused on risk, capabilities, and ESG issues.

These reactionary efforts are born out of buyers' realization that they don't have the information they need about their suppliers. For example, consider what happens if the EU implements a mandatory due diligence duty requiring companies "to identify, prevent, mitigate, and account for sustainability impacts in their operations and supply chains, backed by regulatory enforcement mechanisms." Does the procurement organization know the impact? Does it have this information readily available? Probably not, so the company sends out a deluge of surveys.

Now imagine being that supplier—inundated by every customer they serve sending out risk surveys, sustainability surveys, diversity surveys, capability surveys, forced labor surveys, conflict mineral surveys, human rights surveys, innovation idea surveys, and countless other "please fill out this data request" surveys. This rapidly leads to what can only be termed "initiative fatigue."

Many large enterprises have more than 50,000 suppliers and some as many as 100,000, which raises some uncomfortable questions for buying organizations. If every supplier fills out every survey, what happens with all the information? Does the data serve a strategic purpose, or is this a gigantic check-the-box exercise? What does the company do with this type of data? For example, if a tier 3 supplier has no diversity in its leadership or employee base and has no intention of changing that, what exactly can Acme do about it?

Enter supplier experience management

A supplier's objective is to get business, get paid, and get more business. Everything else is overhead and wasted time. For all the perceived benefits of a supplier portal—and the quantifiable painful downsides—a crucial piece is missing from the discussion. What value are companies giving back to their suppliers? And what might happen if they had a system that put a spotlight on what suppliers need?

Enter supplier experience management (SXM). SXM gives suppliers an easy way to interact with supply chain systems. This is how we make data exchange simple for third-party data exchange. Information exchanged in this manner is syndicated so that any data produced once can be shared across many companies. An SXM system designed to engage suppliers includes the following components:

— **Information management.** There is only one place to enter all the information about a supplier, including address, parent, and subsidiary information, and (most importantly) banking details. It's basically LinkedIn for suppliers.

— **Performance.** This includes qualitative and quantitative feedback about how customers measure, track, and view a supplier.

— **Connectivity.** Third parties should be able to easily connect to systems, such as contracting, bidding, invoicing, quality, collaboration, and catalog management. This extends beyond simply providing a single sign-on to the systems and a launch page; that's just the minimum. Buyers should also use sophisticated intelligence to direct suppliers to where they need to go and, in some cases, tell them what they need to do.

— **Communication.** The overriding question here is how do we avoid confusing suppliers? To effectively communicate with them, take a close look at all modes of communication (including monodirectional, bidirectional, and multiparty) and the frequency, content (including branding), tracking (click-through rates and engagement), and channels (email, social media, and individual tools such as innovation hubs, portals, or in-system communications).

— **Relationship building.** Communications between a supplier and a buying organization should include how much the company is spending with them, how much they're spending with the company, and what else the company could or should be doing with its suppliers.

— **Extensibility.** Third-party collaboration needs to occur outside the corporate's four walls. For example, Acme Company might need to connect its designing, planning, and ERP systems directly to its contract manufacturers and third-party logistics (3PL) providers' systems. From a supplier's perspective, there must be an easy, compelling way to share this information.

— **Support.** Who do suppliers contact when they need help? What if they can't log in? What if an invoice is overdue? Is there a way to chat with someone? If there's an email address, where does it go? Is there a service-level agreement? If so, is it communicated back to the supplier? Is there a ticketing system to track issues?

— **Insights.** Suppliers can benefit from having a comprehensive view of the customer relationship. How much is the supplier selling to a particular company? What kind of activities is the supplier engaged in? If the supplier bids on 100 projects, how many does it win? Is the supplier invited to all the sourcing events where it has capabilities? Are there particular win themes that the supplier is missing?

— **Reduced administrative overhead.** While this is somewhat self-explanatory, the goal is to ensure that suppliers do not have to invest too much effort or money chasing late payments. However, it's important to keep looking for opportunities to uncover SXM issues before they become problematic. For example, proactively monitor invoice aging to catch unpaid invoices, which can be a sign of problems with the contractual terms. Process mining tools can also help streamline and monitor these processes.

Segmenting suppliers for security

Let's say Acme Company has 30,000 suppliers. Not only is this too many to engage with, but it's also far too many to manage effectively. This is where supplier segmentation comes into play. There are a number of traditional models for segmenting suppliers. However, in the digital era, I would like to offer a new approach, using simple numbers to illustrate the point and noting that each company experience will have unique ratios and segmentation criteria.

To start, let's assume that you can effectively engage with 1,000 suppliers on a daily, weekly, or monthly basis. That means the company can offload the bulk of its suppliers—98 percent—to a third-party management platform (onboarding, compliance checks, payments, and so forth). This new category of digital solutions allows companies to offboard non-strategic suppliers, vastly reducing the number of suppliers the company needs to manage in its data management systems.

To identify the 1,000 suppliers, look at the following criteria:

— Capability

— Direct versus indirect

— ESG

— Frequency

— Performance

— Quality

— Risk

— Volume

The most important change is that with the proper digital tools, supplier segmentation can be dynamic. Also, new suppliers can start in the third-party management system. Then as their role changes and they become more important, they can be moved over to the core systems (or vice versa). In other words, suppliers' status—and their engagement levels—will continually change. Having flexible systems will be essential to support this movement.

Where to start

If you want to be the customer of choice for your suppliers, it's time to prove it. What are you doing to show your suppliers that you care about them? What are you doing to make their experience with your company efficient and easy? First and foremost, every buying organization needs to get their supplier information management (SIM) activities under control.

Here are seven ways to get started:

1. Segment your suppliers, such as by region, direct versus indirect, volume, or category.

2. Identify and move your non-strategic suppliers to a third-party management solution.

3. Audit your strategic supplier records to ensure they are complete and design a strategy and execution plan for correcting any deficiencies to ensure long-term viability.

4. Experience your systems from a supplier's point of view. Make note of the pain points and areas for improvement.

5. Map out the types of supplier journeys throughout your systems for the entire supplier life cycle, from event participation and onboarding to sustainment and offboarding.

6. Design a supplier communication matrix and plan.

7. Chart an SXM road map and prioritize the onboarding of new SXM digital solutions.

What's next in third-party management?

So far, we've established that data is the key ingredient to making algorithms work. We have further noted the importance of data exchange with third parties to increase security and resilience. This creates an important question about who owns all this data. As a supplier, if I fill out a risk or ESG survey, that is still my data. But if I provide a list of all my locations or a list of my company's capabilities, whose data is that? What happens when the enterprise that asked for the data or the tech provider who processed the data takes my data and uses it to create or improve a product?

Third-party data management and ownership: digital wallets

I love to shop online. In fact, I *really* love to shop online. I often spend hours looking for vegan food, high-end vegan fashion, and used history books. But the checkout experience—which forces me once again to enter my phone number, email address, billing address, shipping address, and credit card information—is maddening. When I click the checkout button and I see the 24 form fields that ask for information that I'm certain I've already provided, a little voice in my head starts crying.

Over the past few years I've adopted Apple Pay, which streamlines the process significantly. When I see the Apple Pay button all I need to do is click it and my core information is sent to the seller. So easy, so satisfying. But technologically Apple Pay and others are not the final destination. In this scenario, big tech uses and owns my information. They are just making it easier for me to pay because the information is stored in their digital wallets.

Back in 1997, in the early days of the consumer Internet, we had Web 1.0. This was one-directional communication. I posted an e-commerce website and hoped people found it through one of the popular search engines of the time. In the early 2000s, Web 2.0 emerged from the wreckage of the dotcom collapse. Web 2.0 was built upon an idea of bidirectional communication, with platforms like Facebook, Twitter, LinkedIn, and other social media. What made this unique was that these platforms enabled other users to interact with the content by commenting, sharing, and liking it.

These Web 2.0 companies fed that data into their algorithms to amplify the content and bring it to you without you having to ask or search for it. They helped us find former high school friends or rekindle old romantic relationships. Recommendation engines suggested movies we might like or products we might enjoy. And, of course, they also showed us posts that aligned with individual political and ethical views.

Everything up to this point was fine, but then these companies took your data and started selling it. Those companies in turn took our data and made us the products. Web 3.0, while still in its infancy, is changing this dynamic fundamentally. One of the key tenets of Web 3.0 is that we own our data as individuals. Our data (credit cards, banking, electronic health records, contacts, social profiles) will be stored in digital wallets, and we will get to choose when and where to share it. Because shouldn't we be paid for the use of our data? Tim Berners-Lee, inventor of the worldwide web, is one of the leading champions of individuals clawing back their data from the tech giants. As we take control of our own data, it becomes more secure. I doubt any of us really knows how many legitimate websites house our personal data. That means we're relying on countless retailers and websites to keep our data secure. Given the unacceptable number of data breaches, this is clearly a problem of epic proportions. But pulling our data out of those systems and storing it under our own control makes it vastly more secure.[139]

Let's hope that the correlation to managing third-party supply chain data is obvious. Each of the third parties should own their data and our supply chain systems need to accommodate it, just like an online retailer accepts Apple or Google Pay. This step alone would create a huge improvement in data security. It would severely reduce payment fraud attempts. It would incent suppliers to comprehensively share information by providing suppliers with a mechanism to manage it in one location and share it. This would also reduce the complexity of designing ridiculously complicated data management schemas to accommodate every potential third party.

[139] Renjifo, Daniel. "Tim Berners-Lee's Inrupt launches Solid privacy platform." CNN, December 16, 2022. https://www.cnn.com/2022/12/16/tech/tim-berners-lee-inrupt-spc-intl/index.html (Accessed May 11, 2023).